TRADITIONAL ITALIAN RECIPES

2022 EDITION

EASY RECIPES FOR EATING WELL EVERYDAY

SILVIA GRANATA

TABLE OF CONTENTS

Baked Onions

Cipolle al Forno

Makes 4 to 8 servings

These onions turn smooth and sweet when cooked; try them with roast beef.

4 medium white or red onions, peeled

½ cup plain dry bread crumbs

¼ cup freshly grated Parmigiano-Reggiano or Pecorino Romano

2 tablespoons olive oil

Salt and freshly ground black pepper

1. Bring a medium saucepan of water to a boil. Add the onions and reduce the heat so that the water just simmers. Cook 5 minutes. Let the onions cool in the water in the pan. Drain the onions and cut them in half crosswise.

2. Place a rack in the center of the oven. Preheat the oven to 350°F. Oil a baking pan just large enough to hold the onions in a single layer. Place the onions in the pan cut-side up. In a small bowl, mix together the bread crumbs, cheese, olive oil, and salt and pepper to taste. Spoon the bread crumbs on top of the onions.

3. Bake 1 hour or until the onions are golden and tender when pierced with a knife. Serve hot or at room temperature.

Onions with Balsamic Vinegar

Cipolle al Balsamico

Makes 6 servings

Balsamic vinegar complements the sweet flavor and color of red onions. These go well with roast pork or pork chops.

6 medium red onions

6 tablespoons extra-virgin olive oil

3 tablespoons balsamic vinegar

Salt and freshly ground black pepper

1. Place a rack in the center of the oven. Preheat the oven to 375°F. Line a baking pan with foil.

2. Wash the onions, but do not peel them. Place the onions in the prepared pan. Bake the onions 1 hour to $1^1/_2$ hours, until tender when pierced with a knife.

3. Trim off the root ends of the onions and peel off the skin. Cut the onions into quarters and place them in a bowl. Add the oil, vinegar, and salt and pepper to taste, and toss to combine. Serve hot or at room temperature.

Red Onion Confit

Confettura di Cipolle Rosse

Makes about 1 pint

Tropea, on the Calabrian coast, is known for its sweet red onions. Though the red onions in the United States are more pungent, you can still make this delicious jam that we ate at Locanda di Alia in Castrovillari. The jam was served with golden fried sardines, but it is also good with pork chops or grilled chicken. I also like it as a condiment with a sharp cheese, such as aged pecorino.

A variation of the jam includes some chopped fresh mint. Be sure to use a heavy-bottomed saucepan and keep the heat very low to prevent the onions from sticking. Add a little water if they dry out too quickly.

1¼ pounds red onions, very finely chopped

1 cup dry red wine

1 teaspoon salt

2 tablespons unsalted butter

1 tablespoon balsamic vinegar

1 or 2 tablespoons honey

About 1 tablespoon sugar

1. In a medium heavy saucepan, combine the onions, red wine, and salt over medium heat. Bring to a simmer and turn the heat to low. Cover and cook, stirring often, for 1 hour 15 minutes or until the onions are very tender. The onions will be slightly translucent.

2. Stir in the butter, balsamic vinegar, and 1 tablespoon each of the honey and sugar. Cook uncovered, stirring often, until all of the liquid has evaporated and the mixture is very thick.

3. Let cool slightly. Serve at room temperature or slightly warm. This keeps in the refrigerator for up to a month. To reheat, place the confit in a small bowl set over a pan of simmering water, or warm it in a microwave.

Roasted Onion and Beet Salad

Insalata di Cipolla e Barbabietola

Makes 6 servings

If you have never had fresh beets in season, you really should try them. When they are young and tender, they are remarkably sweet and flavorful. Buy them in the summer and fall, when they are at their best. As they age they become woody and tasteless.

6 beets, trimmed and scrubbed

2 large onions, peeled

6 tablespoons olive oil

2 tablespoons red wine vinegar

Salt and freshly ground black pepper

6 fresh basil leaves

1. Place a rack in the center of the oven. Preheat the oven to 400°F. Scrub the beets and wrap them in a large sheet of aluminum foil, sealing tightly. Place the package on a baking sheet.

2. Cut the onions into bite-size pieces. Place them in a baking pan and toss with 2 tablespoons of the olive oil.

3. Place the package of beets and the pan of onions side by side in the oven. Bake 1 hour or until the beets are tender when pierced with a knife and the onions are browned.

4. Let the beets cool. Peel off the skins and cut the beets into wedges.

5. In a large bowl, toss the beets and onions with $^1\!/_4$ cup olive oil, the vinegar, and salt and pepper to taste. Sprinkle with the basil and serve immediately.

Pearl Onions with Honey and Orange

Cipolline Profumate all'Arancia

Makes 8 servings

Sweet and tart pearl onions flavored with honey, orange, and vinegar are good with a holiday turkey or capon, roast pork, or as an appetizer with sliced salumi. You can make them ahead, but they should be reheated gently before serving.

2 pounds pearl onions

1 navel orange

2 tablespoons unsalted butter

$\frac{1}{4}$ cup honey

$\frac{1}{4}$ cup white wine vinegar

Salt and freshly ground black pepper

1. Bring a large pot of water to a boil. Add the onions and cook for 3 minutes. Drain and cool them under running water. With a sharp paring knife, shave off the tip of the root ends. Do not slice off the ends too deeply or the onions will fall apart during cooking. Slip off the skins.

2. With a swivel-blade vegetable peeler, remove the orange zest. Stack the strips of zest and cut them into thin matchsticks. Squeeze the juice from the orange. Set aside.

3. In a large skillet, melt the butter over medium heat. Add the onions and cook 30 minutes or until lightly browned, shaking the pan occasionally so that they do not stick.

4. Add the orange juice, zest, honey, vinegar, and salt and pepper to taste. Turn the heat to low and cook 10 minutes, turning the onions frequently, until the onions are tender when pierced with a knfe and glazed with the sauce. Let cool slightly. Serve warm.

Peas with Onions

Piselli con Cipolle

Makes 4 servings

A little water added to the pan helps the onion to mellow and soften without browning. The sweetness of the onion enhances the flavor of the peas.

2 tablespoons olive oil

1 medium onion, finely chopped

4 tablespoons water

2 cups fresh shelled peas or 1 (10-ounce) package frozen peas

Pinch of dried oregano

Salt

1. Pour the oil into a medium saucepan. Add the onion and 2 tablespoons of the water. Cook, stirring frequently, until the onion is very tender, about 15 minutes.

2. Stir in the peas, the remaining 2 tablespoons of water, the oregano, and the salt. Cover and cook until the peas are tender, 5 to 10 minutes.

Peas with Prosciutto and Green Onions

Piselli al Prosciutto

Makes 4 servings

These peas are good with lamb chops or roast lamb.

3 tablespoons unsalted butter

4 green onions, trimmed and thinly sliced

2 cups fresh shelled peas or 1 (10-ounce) package frozen peas

1 teaspoon sugar

Salt

4 thin slices imported Italian prosciutto, cut crosswise into thin strips

1. Melt 2 tablespoons of the butter in a medium skillet. Add the green onions and cook 1 minute.

2. Add the peas, sugar, and salt to taste. Stir in 2 tablespoons water and cover the pan. Cook over low heat until the peas are tender, 5 to 10 minutes.

3. Stir in the prosciutto and remaining 1 tablespoon of butter.
Cook 1 minute more and serve hot.

Sweet Peas with Lettuce and Mint

Piselli alla Menta

Makes 4 servings

Even frozen peas taste like fresh-picked when they are prepared this way. The lettuce adds a slight crunch and the mint a bright, fresh flavor.

2 tablespoons unsalted butter

¼ cup onion, very finely chopped

2 cups fresh shelled peas or 1 (10-ounce) package frozen peas

1 cup shredded lettuce leaves

12 mint leaves, torn into bits

Salt and freshly ground black pepper

1. In a medium saucepan, melt the butter over medium heat. Add the onion and cook until tender and golden, about 10 minutes.

2. Add the peas, lettuce, mint leaves, and salt and pepper to taste. Stir in 2 tablespoons water and cover the pan. Cook 5 to 10 minutes or until the peas are tender. Serve hot.

Easter Pea Salad

Insalata di Pasqua

Makes 4 servings

In the 1950s Romeo Salta was considered one of the best Italian restaurants in New York City. It stood out because it was very elegant and served northern Italian food at a time when most people were only familiar with family-style restaurants serving the red sauced dishes of the south. The owner, Romeo Salta, had learned the restaurant business by working on luxury cruise liners—at that time, the finest training ground for restaurant personnel. This salad would appear on the menu around Easter, when fresh peas became abundant. The original recipe also contained anchovies, though I prefer the salad without them. Sometimes I add chopped Swiss or a similar cheese along with the prosciutto.

2½ cups fresh shelled peas or 1 (10-ounce) package frozen peas

Salt

1 hard-cooked egg yolk

¼ cup olive oil

¼ cup lemon juice

Freshly ground black pepper

2 ounces sliced imported Italian prosciutto, cut crosswise into narrow strips

1. For either fresh or frozen peas, bring a medium saucepan of water to boiling. Add the peas and salt to taste. Cook until the peas are barely tender, about 3 minutes. Drain the peas. Cool them under cold running water. Blot the peas dry.

2. In a serving bowl, mash the egg yolk with a fork. Whisk in the oil, lemon juice, and salt and pepper to taste. Add the peas and toss gently. Add the prosciutto strips and serve immediately.

Roasted Peppers

Peperoni Arrostiti

Makes 8 servings

Roasted peppers are good in salads, omelets, and sandwiches. They freeze well, too, so you can make a batch in the summer when peppers are plentiful and keep them for winter meals.

8 large red, yellow, or green bell peppers

1. Cover the broiler pan with foil. Place the broiler pan about 3 inches away from the heat source. Place the whole peppers on the pan. Turn on the broiler to high. Broil the peppers, turning them frequently with tongs, about 15 minutes or until the skin blisters and they are charred all over. Put the peppers in a bowl. Cover with foil and let cool.

2. Cut the peppers in half, draining the juices into a bowl. Peel off the skins and discard the seeds and stems.

3. Cut the peppers lengthwise into 1-inch strips and place them in a serving bowl. Strain the juices over the peppers.

4. Serve at room temperature or store in the refrigerator and serve chilled. The peppers keep 3 days in the refrigerator or 3 months in the freezer.

Roasted Pepper Salad

Insalata di Peperoni Arrostiti

Makes 8 servings

Serve these peppers as part of an antipasto assortment, as a side dish with grilled tuna or pork, or as an antipasto with sliced fresh mozzarella.

1 recipe (8 peppers) Roasted Peppers

⅓ cup extra-virgin olive oil

4 basil leaves, torn into bits

2 garlic cloves, thinly sliced

Salt and freshly ground black pepper

Prepare the peppers, if necessary. Toss the peppers with the oil, basil, garlic, and salt and pepper to taste. Let stand 1 hour before serving.

Roasted Peppers with Onions and Herbs

Peperoni Arrostiti con Cipolle

Makes 4 servings

Serve these peppers hot or at room temperature. They also make a good topping for crostini.

$\frac{1}{2}$ recipe Roasted Peppers; use red or yellow bell peppers

1 medium onion, halved and thinly sliced

Pinch of crushed red pepper

2 tablespoons olive oil

Salt

$\frac{1}{2}$ teaspoon dried oregano, crumbled

2 tablespoons chopped fresh flat-leaf parsley

1. Prepare the peppers through step 3, if necessary. Then, drain the peppers and cut them lengthwise into $1/2$-inch strips.

2. In a medium skillet, cook the onion with the crushed red pepper in the oil over medium heat until the onion is tender and golden,

about 10 minutes. Add the peppers, oregano, and salt to taste.
Cook, stirring occasionally, until heated through, about 5
minutes. Stir in the parsley and cook 1 minute more. Serve hot
or at room temperature.

Baked Peppers with Tomatoes

Peperoni al Forno

Makes 4 servings

In this recipe from Abruzzo, a fresh, not-too-hot chile seasons the bell peppers. Crushed red pepper or a small dried chile pepper can be substituted. These peppers are good in a sandwich.

2 large red bell peppers

2 large yellow bell peppers

1 chile, such as jalapeño, seeded and chopped

3 tablespoons olive oil

Salt

2 garlic cloves, chopped

2 medium tomatoes, peeled, seeded, and chopped

1. Place a rack in the center of the oven. Preheat the oven to 400°F. Oil a large baking pan. Stand the peppers on a cutting board. Holding the stem in one hand, place the cutting edge of a large heavy chef's knife just beyond the edge of the cap. Cut straight down. Turn the pepper 90° and cut straight down again. Repeat, turning and cutting the remaining two sides. Discard the core, seeds, and stem, which will be in one piece. Cut away any membranes and scrape out any seeds.

2. Cut the peppers lengthwise into 1-inch strips. Add the chile to the pan. Add the oil and salt to taste and toss well. Spread the peppers out in the pan.

3. Bake the peppers 25 minutes. Add the garlic and tomatoes and stir well. Bake 20 minutes more or until the peppers are tender when pierced with a knife. Serve hot.

Peppers with Balsamic Vinegar

Peperoni al Balsamico

Makes 6 servings

The sweetness of balsamic vinegar complements the sweetness of peppers. Serve these hot with pork or lamb chops or at room temperature with cold chicken or roast pork.

6 large red bell peppers

¼ cup olive oil

Salt and freshly ground black pepper

2 tablespoons balsamic vinegar

1. Place a rack in the center of the oven. Preheat the oven to 400°F. Stand the peppers on a cutting board. Holding the stem in one hand, place the cutting edge of a large heavy chef's knife just beyond the edge of the cap. Cut straight down. Turn the pepper 90° and cut straight down again. Repeat, turning and cutting the remaining two sides. Discard the core, seeds, and stem, which will be in one piece. Cut away any membranes and scrape out any seeds.

2. Cut the peppers into 1-inch strips. Place them in a large shallow roasting pan with the oil and salt and pepper. Toss well. Bake the peppers 30 minutes.

3. Stir in the vinegar. Bake the peppers 20 minutes more or until tender. Serve hot or at room temperature.

Pickled Peppers

Peperoni Sott'Aceto

Makes 2 pints

Colorful peppers packed in vinegar are delicious in sandwiches or with cold meats. These can be used to make the Molise-Style Pepper Sauce.

2 large red bell peppers

2 large yellow bell peppers

Salt

2 cups white wine vinegar

2 cups water

Pinch of crushed red pepper

1. Stand the peppers on a cutting board. Holding the stem in one hand, place the cutting edge of a large heavy chef's knife just beyond the edge of the cap. Cut straight down. Turn the pepper 90° and cut straight down again. Repeat, turning and cutting the remaining two sides. Discard the core, seeds, and stem, which will be in one piece. Cut away any membranes and scrape out any seeds. Cut the peppers lengthwise into 1-inch strips. Place the peppers in a colander set over a plate and sprinkle with salt. Let stand 1 hour to drain.

2. In a nonreactive saucepan, combine the vinegar, water, and crushed red pepper. Bring to a simmer. Remove from the heat and let cool slightly.

3. Rinse the bell peppers under cold water and pat them dry. Pack the peppers in 2 sterilized pint jars. Pour on the cooled vinegar mixture and seal. Let stand in a cool, dark place 1 week before using.

Peppers with Almonds

Peperoni alle Mandorle

Makes 4 servings

An old friend of my mother's whose family came from Ischia, a small island in the bay of Naples, gave her this recipe. She liked to serve it for lunch over slices of Italian bread fried in olive oil until golden.

2 red and 2 yellow bell peppers

1 garlic clove, lightly crushed

3 tablespoons olive oil

2 medium tomatoes, peeled, seeded, and chopped

¼ cup water

2 tablespoons capers

4 anchovy fillets, chopped

4 ounces toasted almonds, coarsely chopped

1. Stand the peppers on a cutting board. Holding the stem in one hand, place the cutting edge of a large heavy chef's knife just beyond the edge of the cap. Cut straight down. Turn the pepper 90° and cut straight down again. Repeat, turning and cutting the remaining two sides. Discard the core, seeds, and stem, which will be in one piece. Cut away any membranes and scrape out any seeds.

2. In a large skillet, cook the garlic with the oil over medium heat, pressing the garlic once or twice with the back of a spoon. As soon as it is lightly browned, about 4 minutes, discard the garlic.

3. Add the peppers to the pan. Cook, stirring often, until softened, about 15 minutes.

4. Add the tomatoes and water. Cook until the sauce is thickened, about 15 minutes more.

5. Stir in the capers, anchovies, and almonds. Taste for salt. Cook 2 minutes more. Let cool slightly before serving.

Peppers with Tomatoes and Onions

Peperonata

Makes 4 servings

Every region seems to have its version of peperonata. Some add capers, olives, herbs, or anchovies. Serve this as a side dish or as a sauce for roast pork or grilled fish.

4 red or yellow bell peppers (or a mix)

2 medium onions, thinly sliced

3 tablespoons olive oil

3 large tomatoes, peeled, seeded, and coarsely chopped

1 garlic clove, finely chopped

Salt

1. Stand the peppers on a cutting board. Holding the stem in one hand, place the cutting edge of a large heavy chef's knife just beyond the edge of the cap. Cut straight down. Turn the pepper 90° and cut straight down again. Repeat, turning and cutting the remaining two sides. Discard the core, seeds, and stem, which will be in one piece. Cut away any membranes and scrape out any seeds. Cut the peppers into $^1/_4$-inch strips.

2. In a large skillet over medium heat, cook the onions in the olive oil until tender and golden, about 10 minutes. Add the pepper strips and cook 10 minutes more.

3. Stir in the tomatoes, garlic, and salt to taste. Cover and cook 20 minutes or until the peppers are tender when pierced with a knife. If there is a lot of liquid remaining, uncover and cook until the sauce is thickened and reduced. Serve hot or at room temperature.

Stuffed Frying Peppers

Peperoni Ripieni

Makes 4 to 8 servings

My grandmother always made these peppers in the summertime. She would cook them in a big black skillet in the morning, and by lunchtime they were just the right temperature for serving with sliced bread.

1¼ cups plain dry bread crumbs made from Italian or French bread

⅓ cup freshly grated Pecorino Romano or Parmigiano-Reggiano

¼ cup chopped fresh flat-leaf parsley

1 garlic clove, finely chopped

Salt and freshly ground black pepper

About ½ cup olive oil

8 long light-green Italian frying peppers

3 cups peeled, seeded, and chopped fresh tomatoes or 1 (28-ounce) can crushed tomatoes

6 fresh basil leaves, torn into bits

1. In a bowl, mix together the bread crumbs, cheese, parsley, garlic, and salt and pepper to taste. Stir in 3 tablespoons of the oil, or enough to moisten the crumbs evenly.

2. Cut off the tops of the peppers and scoop out the seeds. Spoon the bread crumb mixture into the peppers, leaving about 1 inch of clearance at the top. Do not overstuff the peppers, or the filling will spill out as the peppers cook.

3. In a large skillet, heat $1/4$ cup of oil over medium heat until a piece of pepper sizzles in the pan. With tongs, add the peppers carefully. Cook, turning occasionally with tongs, until browned on all sides, about 20 minutes.

4. Pour the tomatoes, basil, and salt and pepper to taste around the peppers. Bring to a simmer. Cover and cook, turning the peppers once or twice, until very tender, about 15 minutes. If the sauce is too dry, add a little water. Uncover and cook until the sauce is thick, about 5 minutes more. Serve warm or at room temperature.

Neapolitan-Style Stuffed Peppers

Peperoni alla Nonna

Makes 6 servings

If Sicilians have countless ways to cook eggplants, Neapolitans have the same creativity with peppers. This is another typical Neapolitan recipe that my grandmother used to make.

2 medium eggplants (about 1 pound each)

6 large red, yellow, or green bell peppers, cut into ½-inch strips

½ cup plus 3 tablespoons olive oil

3 medium tomatoes, peeled, seeded, and chopped

¾ cup pitted and chopped mild, oil-cured black olives, such as Gaeta

6 anchovy fillets, finely chopped

3 tablespoons capers, rinsed and drained

1 large garlic clove, peeled and finely chopped

3 tablespoons chopped fresh flat-leaf parsley

Freshly ground black pepper

½ cup plus 1 tablespoon plain bread crumbs

1. Trim the eggplants and cut them into ³/₄-inch cubes. Layer the pieces in a colander, sprinkling each layer with salt. Place the colander over a plate and let drain for 1 hour. Rinse the eggplant and pat dry with paper towels.

2. In a large skillet, heat the ¹/₂ cup of oil over medium heat. Add the eggplant and cook, stirring occasionally, until tender, about 10 minutes.

3. Stir in the tomatoes, olives, anchovies, capers, garlic, parsley, and pepper to taste. Bring to a simmer, then cook 5 minutes more. Stir in the ¹/₂ cup of bread crumbs and remove from the heat.

4. Place a rack in the center of the oven. Preheat the oven to 450°F. Oil a baking pan just large enough to hold the peppers upright.

5. Cut off the stems of the peppers and remove the seeds and white membranes. Stuff the eggplant mixture into the peppers. Stand the peppers in the prepared pan. Sprinkle with the remaining 1 tablespoon bread crumbs and drizzle with the remaining 3 tablespoons oil.

6. Pour 1 cup water around the peppers. Bake 1 hour 15 minutes or until the peppers are very tender and lightly browned. Serve hot or at room temperature.

Stuffed Peppers, Ada Boni's Style

Peperoni Ripieni alla Ada Boni

Makes 4 to 8 servings

Ada Boni was a famous Italian food writer and the author of numerous cookbooks. Her Italian Regional Cooking is a classic, and one of the first books on the subject translated into English. This recipe is adapted from the Sicily chapter.

4 medium red or yellow bell peppers

1 cup toasted plain bread crumbs

4 tablespoons raisins

$\frac{1}{2}$ cup chopped pitted mild black olives

6 anchovy fillets, chopped

2 tablespoons chopped fresh basil

2 tablespoons capers, rinsed, drained, and chopped

$\frac{1}{4}$ cup plus 2 tablespoons olive oil

1 cup Sicilian Tomato Sauce

1. Place a rack in the center of the oven. Preheat the oven to 375°F. Oil a 13 × 9 × 2-inch baking dish.

2. With a large heavy chef's knife, cut the peppers in half lengthwise. Cut out the stems, seeds, and white membranes.

3. In a large bowl, mix together the bread crumbs, raisins, olives, anchovies, basil, capers, and $1/4$ cup of the oil. Taste and adjust seasoning. (Salt will probably be unnecessary.)

4. Spoon the mixture into the pepper halves. Top with the sauce. Bake 50 minutes or until the peppers are very tender when pierced with a knife. Serve hot or at room temperature.

Fried Peppers

Peperoni Fritti

Makes 6 to 8 servings

Crisp and sweet, these are hard to resist. Serve them with an omelet or with any cooked meat.

4 large red or yellow bell peppers

½ cup all-purpose flour

Salt

1. Stand the peppers on a cutting board. Holding the stem in one hand, place the cutting edge of a large heavy chef's knife just beyond the edge of the cap. Cut straight down. Turn the pepper 90° and cut straight down again. Repeat, turning and cutting the remaining two sides. Discard the core, seeds, and stem, which will be in one piece. Cut away any membranes and scrape out any seeds. Cut the peppers into $1/4$-inch strips.

2. Heat about 2 inches of oil in a deep heavy saucepan until the temperature reaches 375°F on a frying thermometer.

3. Line a tray with paper towels. Put the flour in a shallow bowl. Roll the pepper strips in the flour, shaking off the excess.

4. Add the peppers strips to the hot oil a few at a time. Fry until golden and tender, about 4 minutes. Drain on the paper towels. Fry the remainder in batches, in the same way. Sprinkle with salt and serve immediately.

Sautéed Peppers with Zucchini and Mint

Peperoni e Zucchini in Padella

Makes 6 servings

The longer this sits, the better it tastes, so make it early in the day to serve for a later meal.

1 red bell pepper

1 yellow bell pepper

2 tablespoons olive oil

4 small zucchini, cut into ¼-inch slices

Salt

2 tablespoons white wine vinegar

2 garlic cloves, very finely chopped

2 tablespoons chopped fresh mint

½ teaspoon dried oregano

Pinch of crushed red pepper

1. Stand the peppers on a cutting board. Holding the stem in one hand, place the cutting edge of a large heavy chef's knife just beyond the edge of the cap. Cut straight down. Turn the pepper 90° and cut straight down again. Repeat, turning and cutting the remaining two sides. Discard the core, seeds, and stem, which will be in one piece. Cut away any membranes and scrape out any seeds. Cut the peppers into 1-inch strips.

2. In a large skillet, heat the oil over medium heat. Add the peppers and cook, stirring, for 10 minutes.

3. Add the zucchini and salt to taste. Cook, stirring often, until the zucchini are tender, about 15 minutes.

4. While the vegetables are cooking, in a medium bowl, whisk together the vinegar, garlic, herbs, red pepper, and salt to taste.

5. Stir in the peppers and zucchini. Let stand until the vegetables are at room temperature. Taste and adjust seasoning.

Roasted Pepper and Eggplant Terrine

Sformato di Peperoni e Melanzane

Makes 8 to 12 servings

This is an unusual and beautiful terrine of layered peppers, eggplant, and flavorings. The pepper juices gel slightly after chilling and hold the terrine together. Serve it as a first course or as a side dish with grilled meats.

4 large red bell peppers, roasted and peeled

2 large eggplants (about 1½ pounds each)

Salt

Olive oil

½ cup torn fresh basil leaves

4 large garlic cloves, peeled, seeded, and finely chopped

¼ cup red wine vinegar

Freshly ground black pepper

1. Prepare the peppers, if necessary. Trim the eggplants and cut them lengthwise into ¹/₄-inch-thick slices. Layer the slices in a colander, sprinkling each layer with salt. Let stand at least 30 minutes.

2. Preheat the oven to 450°F. Brush two large jelly roll pans with oil.

3. Rinse the eggplant slices in cool water and pat dry with paper towels. Arrange the eggplant in the pans in a single layer. Brush with oil. Bake the eggplant about 10 minutes, until lightly browned on top. Turn the pieces with tongs and bake about 10 minutes more or until tender and lightly browned.

4. Drain the peppers and cut them into 1-inch strips.

5. Line an 8 × 4 × 3–inch loaf pan with plastic wrap. Place a layer of eggplant slices in the bottom of the pan, overlapping them slightly. Make a layer of the roasted peppers over the eggplant. Sprinkle with some of the basil, garlic, vinegar, oil, and salt and pepper to taste. Continue layering, pressing each layer down firmly, until all of the ingredients are used. Cover with plastic wrap and weight the contents with a second loaf pan filled with heavy cans. Refrigerate for at least 24 hours or up to 3 days.

6. To serve, uncover the terrine and invert it onto a serving place. Carefully remove the plastic wrap. Cut the terrine into thick slices. Serve cold or at room temperature.

Sweet-and-Sour Potatoes

Patate in Agrodolce

Makes 6 to 8 servings

This is a Sicilian-style potato salad to serve at room temperature with grilled pork ribs, chicken, or sausages.

2 pounds all-purpose potatoes, such as Yukon gold

1 onion

2 tablespoons olive oil

1 cup pitted mild black olives, such as Gaeta

2 tablespoons capers

Salt and freshly ground black pepper

2 tablespoons white wine vinegar

2 tablespoons sugar

1. Scrub the potatoes with a brush under cold running water. Peel them if desired. Cut the potatoes into halves or quarters if large.

In a large skillet, cook the onion in the oil until tender and golden, about 10 minutes.

2. Stir in the potatoes, olives, capers, and salt and pepper to taste. Add 1 cup of water and bring to a simmer. Cook 15 minutes.

3. In a small bowl, stir together the vinegar and sugar, and add it to the skillet. Continue to cook until the potatoes are tender, about 5 minutes. Remove from the heat and let cool completely. Serve at room temperature.

Potatoes with Balsamic Vinegar

Patate al Balsamico

Makes 6 servings

Red onion and balsamic vinegar flavor these potatoes. They are good at room temperature, too.

2 pounds all-purpose potatoes, such as Yukon gold

2 tablespoons olive oil

1 large red onion, chopped

2 tablespoons water

Salt and freshly ground black pepper

2 tablespoons balsamic vinegar

1. Scrub the potatoes with a brush under cold running water. Peel them if desired. Cut the potatoes into halves or quarters if large.

2. Heat the oil in a medium saucepan over medium heat. Add the potatoes, onion, water, and salt and pepper to taste. Cover the pan and reduce the heat to low. Cook 20 minutes or until the potatoes are tender.

3. Uncover the pan and stir in the vinegar. Cook until most of the liquid evaporates, about 5 minutes. Serve hot or at room temperature.

Venetian-Style Potatoes

Patate alla Veneziana

Makes 4 servings

Though I use Yukon gold potatoes for most cooking, there are many other good varieties available, especially at farmer's markets, and they add variety to potato dishes. Yellow Finn potatoes are good for roasting and baking, and Red Russians are excellent in salads. Though odd looking, blue potatoes can be very good too.

1¼ pounds all-purpose potatoes, such as Yukon gold

2 tablespoons unsalted butter

1 tablespoon olive oil

1 medium onion, chopped

Salt and freshly ground black pepper

2 tablespoons chopped fresh flat-leaf parsley

1. Scrub the potatoes with a brush under cold running water. Peel them if desired. Cut the potatoes into halves or quarters if large. In a large skillet, melt the butter with the oil over medium heat. Add the onion and cook until softened, about 5 minutes.

2. Add the potatoes and salt and pepper to taste. Cover the pan
and cook, stirring occasionally, about 20 minutes, or until the
potatoes are tender.

3. Add the parsley and stir well. Serve hot.

"Jumped" Potatoes

Patate al Salto

Makes 4 servings

When you order fried potatoes in an Italian restaurant, this is what you get. The potatoes become lightly crusty on the outside and soft and creamy inside. They are called "jumped" potatoes because they need frequent stirring or tossing in the pan.

1¼ pounds all-purpose potatoes, such as Yukon gold

¼ cup olive oil

Salt and freshly ground black pepper

1. Scrub the potatoes with a brush under cold running water. Peel the potatoes. Cut them into 1-inch pieces.

2. Pour the oil into a 9-inch skillet. Place the pan over medium-high heat until the oil is very hot and a piece of potato sizzles when added.

3. Dry the potatoes well with paper towels. Add the potatoes to the hot oil and let cook 2 minutes. Turn the potatoes and cook 2 minutes more. Continue cooking and turning the potatoes every

2 minutes or until lightly browned on all sides, about 10 minutes in all.

4. Add salt and pepper to taste. Cover the pan and cook, turning occasionally, until the potatoes are tender when pierced with a knife, about 5 minutes. Serve immediately.

Variation: *Potatoes with Garlic and Herbs*: In step 4 add 2 garlic cloves, chopped, and a tablespoon of chopped fresh rosemary or sage.

Potato-Pepper Sauté

Patate e Peperoni in Padella

Makes 6 servings

Peppers, garlic, and hot red pepper flavor this tasty sauté.

1¼ pounds all-purpose potatoes, such as Yukon gold

4 tablespoons olive oil

2 large red or yellow bell peppers, cut into 1-inch pieces

Salt

¼ cup chopped fresh flat-leaf parsley

2 large garlic cloves

Pinch of crushed red pepper

1. Scrub the potatoes with a brush under cold running water. Peel the potatoes and cut them into 1-inch pieces.

2. In a large skillet, heat 2 tablespoons of the oil over medium heat. Dry the potatoes well with paper towels and place them in the pan. Cook, stirring the potatoes from time to time, until they begin to turn brown, about 10 minutes. Sprinkle with salt. Cover the pan and cook 10 minutes.

3. While the potatoes cook, in another skillet, heat the remaining 2 tablespoons oil over medium heat. Add the bell peppers and salt to taste. Cook, stirring occasionally, until the peppers are almost tender, about 10 minutes.

4. Stir the potatoes, then add the peppers. Stir in the parsley, garlic, and crushed red pepper. Cook until the potatoes are tender, about 5 minutes. Serve hot.

Mashed Potatoes with Parsley and Garlic

Patate Schiacciate all'Aglio e Prezzemolo

Makes 4 servings

Mashed potatoes get an Italian treatment with parsley, garlic, and olive oil. If you like your potatoes spicy, stir in a big pinch of crushed red pepper.

1¼ pounds all-purpose potatoes, such as Yukon gold

Salt

¼ cup olive oil

1 large garlic clove, finely chopped

1 tablespoon chopped fresh flat-leaf parsley

Freshly ground black pepper

1. Scrub the potatoes with a brush under cold running water. Peel the potatoes and cut them into quarters. Place the potatoes in a medium saucepan with cold water to cover and salt to taste. Cover and bring to a simmer. Cook 15 minutes or until the potatoes are tender when pierced with a knife. Drain the potatoes, reserving some of the water.

2. Dry the pan in which the potatoes were cooked. Add 2 tablespoons of the oil and the garlic and cook over medium heat until the garlic is just fragrant, about 1 minute. Add the potatoes and parsley to the pan. Mash the potatoes with a masher or a fork, stirring them well to blend them with the garlic and parsley. Add the remaining oil, and salt and pepper to taste. Add a little of the cooking water if needed. Serve immediately.

Variation: *Mashed Potatoes with Olives*: Stir in 2 tablespoons chopped black or green olives just before serving.

Herbed New Potatoes with Pancetta

Patatine alle Erbe Aromatiche

Makes 4 servings

Little new potatoes are delicious cooked this way. (New potatoes are not a variety. Any freshly dug potato with thin skin can be called a new potato.) Use an all-purpose potato if new potatoes are not available.

1¼ pounds small new potatoes

2 ounces sliced pancetta, diced

1 medium onion, chopped

2 tablespoons olive oil

1 garlic clove, finely chopped

6 fresh basil leaves, torn into bits

1 teaspoon chopped fresh rosemary

1 bay leaf

Salt and freshly ground black pepper

1. Scrub the potatoes with a brush under cold running water. Peel them if desired. Cut the potatoes into 1-inch pieces.

2. Combine the pancetta, onion, and olive oil in a large skillet. Cook over medium heat until softened, about 5 minutes.

3. Add the potatoes and cook, stirring occasionally, for 10 minutes.

4. Stir in the garlic, basil, rosemary, bay leaf, and salt and pepper to taste. Cover the pan and cook for 20 minutes more, stirring occasionally, until the potatoes are tender when pierced with a fork. Add a little water if the potatoes begin to brown too rapidly.

5. Remove the bay leaf and serve hot.

Potatoes with Tomatoes and Onions

Patate alla Pizzaiola

Makes 6 to 8 servings.

Potatoes roasted with pizza flavors are typical in Naples and elsewhere in the south.

2 pounds all-purpose potatoes, such as Yukon gold

2 large tomatoes, peeled, seeded, and chopped

2 medium onions, sliced

1 garlic clove, finely chopped

½ teaspoon dried oregano

¼ cup olive oil

Salt and freshly ground black pepper

1. Preheat the oven to 450°F. Scrub the potatoes with a brush under cold running water. Peel them if desired. Cut the potatoes into 1-inch pieces. In a baking pan large enough to hold the ingredients in a single layer, toss together the potatoes, tomatoes, onions, garlic, oregano, oil, and salt and pepper to taste. Spread the ingredients out evenly in the pan.

2. Place a rack in the center of the oven. Roast the vegetables, stirring 2 or 3 times, for 1 hour or until the potatoes are cooked through. Serve hot.

Roasted Potatoes with Garlic and Rosemary

Patate Arrosto

Makes 4 servings

I can never make enough of these crusty brown potatoes. No one can resist them. The trick to making them is to use a pan large enough so that the potato pieces are barely touching and not piled on top of one another. If your roasting pan is not large enough, use a 15 × 10 × 1–inch jelly roll pan, or use two smaller pans.

2 pounds all-purpose potatoes, such as Yukon gold

¼ cup olive oil

1 tablespoon chopped fresh rosemary

Salt and freshly ground black pepper

2 garlic cloves, finely chopped

1. Place a rack in the center of the oven. Preheat the oven to 400°F. Scrub the potatoes with a brush under cold running water. Peel them if desired. Cut the potatoes into 1-inch pieces. Dry the potatoes with paper towels. Put them in a roasting pan large enough to hold the potatoes in a single layer. Drizzle with the oil

and toss with the rosemary and salt and pepper to taste. Spread
the potatoes out evenly.

2. Roast the potatoes, stirring every 15 minutes, for 45 minutes.
Stir in the garlic and cook 15 minutes more or until the potatoes
are tender. Serve hot.

Roasted Potatoes with Mushrooms

Patate e Funghi al Forno

Makes 6 servings

The potatoes pick up some of the mushroom and garlic aromas as they roast in the same pan.

1½ pounds all-purpose potatoes, such as Yukon gold

1 pound mushrooms, any kind, halved or quartered if large

¼ cup olive oil

2 to 3 garlic cloves, thinly sliced

Salt and freshly ground black pepper

2 tablespoons chopped fresh flat-leaf parsley

1. Place a rack in the center of the oven. Preheat the oven to 400°F. Scrub the potatoes with a brush under cold running water. Peel them if desired. Cut the potatoes into 1-inch pieces. Place the potatoes and mushrooms in a large roasting pan. Toss the vegetables with the oil, garlic, and a generous sprinkle of salt and pepper.

2. Roast the vegetables 15 minutes. Toss them well. Bake 30 minutes more, stirring occasionally, or until the potatoes are tender. Sprinkle with chopped parsley and serve hot.

Potatoes and Cauliflower, Basilicata Style

Patate e Cavolfiore al Forno

Makes 4 to 6

Put a pan of potatoes and cauliflower in the oven alongside a roast pork or chicken for a fine Sunday dinner. The vegetables should be crisp and brown around the edges, their flavors enhanced by the perfume of the oregano.

1 small cauliflower

¼ cup olive oil

3 medium all-purpose potatoes, such as Yukon gold quartered

½ teaspoon dried oregano, crumbled

Salt and freshly ground black pepper

1. Cut the cauliflower into 2-inch florets. Trim off the ends of the stems. Cut thick stems crosswise into $1/4$-inch slices.

2. Place a rack in the center of the oven. Preheat the oven to 400°F. Pour the oil into a 13 × 9 × 2– inch roasting pan. Add the vegetables and toss well. Sprinkle with the oregano and salt and pepper to taste. Toss again.

3. Bake 45 minutes or until the vegetables are tender and browned. Serve hot.

Potatoes and Cabbage in the Pan

Patate e Cavolo in Tegame

Makes 4 to 6 servings

Versions of this dish exist all over Italy. In Friuli, smoked pancetta is added to the skillet with the onion. I like this simple version from Basilicata. The pale pink of the onion complements the creamy white potatoes and green cabbage. The potatoes become so soft that they are like mashed potatoes by the time the cabbage is tender.

3 tablespoons olive oil

1 medium red onion, chopped

½ head medium cabbage, thinly sliced (about 4 cups)

3 medium all-purpose potatoes, such as Yukon gold, peeled and cut into bite-size pieces

½ cup water

Salt and freshly ground black pepper

1. Pour the oil into a large skillet. Add the onion and cook over medium heat, stirring frequently, until softened, about 5 minutes.

2. Stir in the cabbage, potatoes, water, and salt and pepper to taste. Cover and cook, stirring occasionally, 30 minutes or until the vegetables are soft. Add a little more water if the vegetables begin to stick. Serve hot.

Potato and Spinach Torte

Torta di Patate e Spinaci

Makes 8 servings

When I had this layered vegetable torte in Rome, it was made with chicory instead of spinach. Roman chicory looks something like young dandelion or mature arugula. Spinach is a good stand-in for the chicory. For best flavor, be sure to let this dish cool slightly before serving it.

2 pounds all-purpose potatoes, such as Yukon gold

Salt

4 tablespoons unsalted butter

1 small onion, very finely chopped

1½ pounds spinach, chicory, dandelion, or Swiss chard, trimmed

½ cup water

½ cup hot milk

1 cup freshly grated Parmigiano-Reggiano

Freshly ground black pepper

1 tablespoon plain bread crumbs

1. Scrub the potatoes with a brush under cold running water. Peel the potatoes and place them in a medium pot with cold water to cover. Add salt and cover the pot. Bring to a boil and cook about 20 minutes, or until the potatoes are tender.

2. In a small skillet, melt 2 tablespoons of the butter over medium heat. Add the onion and cook, stirring often, until the onion is tender and golden.

3. Place the spinach in a large pot with the $1/2$ cup of water and salt to taste. Cover and cook until tender, about 5 minutes. Drain well and squeeze out the excess liquid. Chop the spinach on a board.

4. Add the spinach to the skillet and stir it together with the onion.

5. When the potatoes are tender, drain them and mash them until smooth. Stir in the remaining 2 tablespoons of butter and the milk. Add $3/4$ cup of the cheese and mix well. Season to taste with salt and pepper.

6. Place a rack in the center of the oven. Preheat the oven to 375°F.

7. Generously butter a 9-inch baking dish. Spread half the potatoes
in the dish. Make a second layer of all of the spinach. Top with
the remaining potatoes. Sprinkle with the remaining $^1/_4$ cup of
cheese and the bread crumbs.

8. Bake 45 to 50 minutes or until the top is golden. Let rest 15
minutes before serving.

Neapolitan Potato Croquettes

Panzerotti or Crocche

Makes about 24

In Naples, pizzerias set up sidewalk stands to sell these tasty logs of mashed potatoes in a crisp bread-crumb jacket, making them easy for passersby to eat for lunch or a snack. This, however, is my grandmother's recipe. We ate potato croquettes for holidays and festive occasions all year round, usually as a side dish with roast beef.

2½ pounds all-purpose potatoes, such as Yukon gold

3 large eggs

1 cup freshly grated Pecorino Romano or Parmigiano-Reggiano

2 tablespoons chopped fresh flat-leaf parsley

¼ cup finely chopped salame (about 2 ounces)

Salt and freshly ground black pepper

2 cups plain dry bread crumbs

Vegetable oil for frying

1. Scrub the potatoes with a brush under cold running water. Place the potatoes in a large saucepan with cold water to cover. Cover the pan and bring the water to a boil. Cook over medium heat until the potatoes are tender when pierced with a fork, about 20 minutes. Drain the potatoes, then let them cool slightly. Peel the potatoes. Put them in a large bowl and mash them with a masher or fork until smooth.

2. Separate the eggs, putting the yolks in a small bowl and setting the whites aside in a shallow dish. Spread the bread crumbs on a sheet of wax paper.

3. Stir the egg yolks, cheese, parsley, and salame into the mashed potatoes. Add salt and pepper to taste.

4. Using about $1/4$ cup of the potato mixture, form a sausage shape about 1 inch wide and $2^1/_2$ inches long. Repeat with the remaining potatoes.

5. Beat the egg whites with a whisk or a fork until frothy. Dip the potato logs into the whites, then roll them in the crumbs, coating them completely. Place the logs on a wire rack and let dry 15 to 30 minutes.

6. Pour about $1/2$ inch of the oil into a large heavy skillet. Heat over medium heat until a bit of the egg white sizzles when dropped in

the oil. Carefully place some of the logs in the pan, leaving a little
space between them. Fry them, turning occasionally with tongs,
until evenly browned, about 10 minutes. Transfer the browned
croquettes to paper towels to drain.

7. Serve immediately or keep the croquettes warm in a low oven
while frying the remainder.

Dad's Neapolitan Potato Pie

Gatto'

Makes 6 to 8 servings

Gatto' comes from the French gateau, meaning "cake." The derivation leads me to think this recipe was made popular by the French-trained monzu—chefs who cooked for the aristocrats at the court of Naples.

In our house, we called this potato pie, and if we weren't having potato croquettes with our Sunday dinner, we had this potato dish, which was my father's specialty.

2½ pounds all-purpose potatoes, such as Yukon gold

Salt

¼ cup plain dry bread crumbs

4 tablespoons (½ stick) unsalted butter, softened

1 cup warm milk

1 cup plus 2 tablespoons freshly grated Parmigiano-Reggiano

1 large egg, beaten

¼ teaspoon freshly grated nutmeg

Salt and freshly ground black pepper

8 ounces fresh mozzarella, chopped

4 ounces salame or imported Italian prosciutto, chopped

1. Scrub the potatoes with a brush under cold running water. Place the potatoes in a large saucepan with cold water to cover. Add salt to taste. Cover the pan and bring the water to a boil. Cook over medium heat until the potatoes are tender when pierced with a fork, about 20 minutes. Drain and let cool slightly.

2. Place a rack in the center of the oven. Preheat the oven to 400°F. Butter a 2-quart baking dish. Sprinkle with the bread crumbs.

3. Peel the potatoes, put them in a large bowl, and mash them with a masher or fork until smooth. Stir in 3 tablespoons of the butter, the milk, 1 cup of the Parmigiano, the egg, nutmeg, and salt and pepper to taste. Fold in the mozzarella and salame.

4. Spread the mixture evenly in the prepared dish. Sprinkle with the remaining Parmigiano. Dot with the remaining 1 tablespoon butter.

5. Bake 35 to 45 minutes or until the top is browned. Let stand briefly at room temperature before serving.

Skillet Tomatoes

Pomodori in Padella

Makes 6 to 8 servings

Serve these as a side dish with grilled or roasted meats, or at room temperature, mashed onto toasted country bread as an appetizer.

8 plum tomatoes

$\frac{1}{4}$ cup olive oil

2 garlic cloves, finely chopped

2 tablespoons chopped fresh basil

Salt and freshly ground black pepper

1. Rinse the tomatoes and pat dry. With a small knife, cut around the stem end of each tomato and remove it. Cut the tomatoes in half lengthwise.

2. In a large skillet, heat the oil with the garlic and basil over medium heat. Add the tomato halves cut-side down. Sprinkle with salt and pepper. Cook until the tomatoes are browned and tender, about 10 minutes. Serve hot or at room temperature.

Steamed Tomatoes

Pomodori al Vapore

Makes 4 servings

Here, sweet little tomatoes are cooked in their own juices. Serve them as a side dish with meat or fish, or spoon them over a frittata. If the tomatoes are not quite sweet enough, add a pinch of sugar as they cook.

1 pint cherry or grape tomatoes

2 tablespoons extra-virgin olive oil

Salt

6 basil leaves, stacked and cut into narrow strips

1. Rinse the tomatoes and pat dry. Cut them in half through the stem end. In a small saucepan, combine the tomatoes, oil, and salt. Cover the pan and place on low heat. Cook 10 minutes or until the tomatoes are just softened but still hold their shape.

2. Add the basil. Serve hot or at room temperature.

Baked Tomatoes

Pomodori al Forno

Makes 8 servings

A bread-crumb topping seasons these tomatoes. They are good with roasted fish and most egg dishes.

8 plum tomatoes

1 cup bread crumbs

4 anchovy fillets, finely chopped

2 tablespoons capers, rinsed and drained

½ cup freshly grated Pecorino Romano

½ teaspoon dried oregano

3 tablespoons olive oil

Salt and freshly ground black pepper

1. Rinse and dry the tomatoes. Cut the tomatoes in half lengthwise. With a small spoon, scoop out the seeds into a fine-mesh strainer set over a bowl to collect the juices. In a large skillet, toast the bread crumbs over medium heat, stirring often, until they are just fragrant, not browned, about 5 minutes. Remove from the heat and let cool slightly.

2. Place a rack in the center of the oven. Preheat the oven to 400°F. Oil a large baking pan. Arrange the tomato shells cut-side up in the pan.

3. To the bowl with the tomato juice, add the bread crumbs, anchovies, capers, cheese, oregano, and salt and pepper. Stir in 2 tablespoons of the olive oil. Stuff the mixture into the tomato shells. Drizzle with the remaining tablespoon of oil.

4. Bake 40 minutes or until the tomatoes are tender and the crumbs are golden. Serve hot.

Tomatoes Stuffed with Farro

Pomodori Ripieni

Makes 4 servings

Farro, an ancient grain that is popular in Italy, makes a great stuffing for tomatoes when mixed with cheese and onion. I had something like this at L'Angolo Divino, a wine bar in Rome.

1 cup semipearled farro (or substitute wheat berries or bulgur)

Salt

4 large round tomatoes

1 small onion, finely chopped

2 tablespoons olive oil

¼ cup grated Pecorino Romano or Parmigiano-Reggiano

Freshly ground black pepper

1. In a medium saucepan, bring 4 cups of water to a boil. Add the farro and salt to taste. Cook until the farro is tender but still chewy, about 30 minutes. Drain the farro and place it in a bowl.

2. In a small saucepan, cook the onion in the oil over medium heat until golden, about 10 minutes.

3. Place a rack in the center of the oven. Preheat the oven to 350°F. Oil a small baking pan just large enough to hold the tomatoes.

4. Rinse and dry the tomatoes. Cut a slice $1/2$ inch thick from the top of each tomato and reserve. With a small spoon, scoop out the insides of the tomatoes and place the pulp in a fine-mesh strainer set over a bowl. Arrange the tomato shells in the baking dish.

5. To the bowl with the farro, add the strained tomato liquid, sautéed onion, cheese, and salt and pepper to taste. Spoon the mixture into the tomato shells. Cover the tomatoes with the reserved tops.

6. Bake 20 minutes or until the tomatoes are tender. Serve hot or at room temperature.

Roman Stuffed Tomatoes

Pomodori Ripieni alla Romana

Makes 6 servings

This is a classic Roman dish, typically eaten at room temperature as a first course.

¾ cup medium-grain rice, such as Arborio, Carnaroli, or Vialone Nano

Salt

6 large round tomatoes

4 tablespoons olive oil

3 anchovy fillets, finely chopped

1 small garlic clove, finely chopped

¼ cup chopped fresh basil

¼ cup freshly grated Parmigiano-Reggiano

1. Bring 1 quart of water to a boil over high heat. Add the rice and
   1 teaspoon salt. Reduce the heat to low and simmer for 10

minutes or until the rice is partially cooked but still very firm. Drain well. Put the rice in a large bowl.

2. Place a rack in the center of the oven. Preheat the oven to 350°F. Oil a baking pan just large enough to hold the tomatoes.

3. Cut a $^1/_2$-inch slice from the top of the tomatoes and reserve. With a small spoon, scoop out the insides of the tomatoes and place the pulp in a fine-mesh strainer set over a bowl. Place the tomato shells in the pan.

4. To the bowl with the rice, add the strained tomato liquid and the oil, anchovies, garlic, basil, cheese, and salt to taste. Stir well. Spoon the mixture into the tomato shells. Cover the tomatoes with the reserved tops.

5. Bake 20 minutes or until the rice is tender. Serve hot or at room temperature.

Roasted Tomatoes with Balsamic Vinegar

Pomodori al Balsamico

Makes 6 servings

Balsamic vinegar has a nearly magical way of enhancing the flavor of vegetables. Try this simple dish and serve it as an appetizer or with meats.

8 plum tomatoes

2 tablespoons olive oil

1 tablespoon balsamic vinegar

Salt and freshly ground black pepper

1. Place a rack in the center of the oven. Preheat the oven to 375°F. Oil a baking dish large enough to hold the tomatoes in a single layer.

2. Rinse the tomatoes and pat dry. Cut the tomatoes in half lengthwise. Scoop out the tomato seeds. Place the tomato halves cut-sides up in the pan. Drizzle with the oil and vinegar and sprinkle with salt and pepper.

3. Bake the tomatoes 45 minutes or until tender. Serve at room temperature.

ZUCCHINI AND WINTER SQUASH

Practically every part of the zucchini plant is edible. Sicilians make soup out of the green leaves and vines, known as *tenerumi*. Zucchini and other large squash flowers are stuffed with meat or cheese and fried or poached. The zucchini themselves are used in countless preparations.

Occasionally, I find pale green *romanesco* zucchini in my farmer's market. These are more flavorful than the familiar dark green variety and less watery. The most important thing about zucchini is to choose the smallest ones you can find. They have fewer and more tender seeds and more flavor. The gigantic zucchini generous gardeners are always trying to foist on unsuspecting friends are watery and all but useless.

Winter squashes are sold by the slice in Italy. The varieties used there are often very large, but their texture is similar to the hard squashes found in the United States. Most of the time I rely on butternut squash, which are sweet and buttery, though acorn, Hubbard, or pumpkin can also be used.

Zucchini Carpaccio

Carpaccio in Giallo e Verde

Makes 4 servings

I first ate a simpler version of this refreshing salad at the home of winemaker friends in Tuscany. Over the years, I have embellished it by using a combination of yellow and green zucchini and adding fresh mint.

2 or 3 small zucchini, preferably a mix of yellow and green

3 tablespoons fresh lemon juice

⅓ cup extra-virgin olive oil

Salt and freshly ground black pepper

2 tablespoons finely chopped fresh mint

About 2 ounces Parmigiano-Reggiano, in 1 piece

1. Scrub the zucchini with a brush under cold running water. Trim off the ends.

2. In a food processor or on a mandoline slicer, cut the zucchini into very thin slices. Place the slices in a medium bowl.

3. In a small bowl, whisk together the lemon juice, olive oil, and salt and pepper to taste until blended. Stir in the mint. Drizzle over the zucchini and toss well. Spread the slices out on a shallow platter.

4. With a vegetable peeler, shave the Parmigiano into thin slices. Scatter the slices over the zucchini. Serve immediately.

Zucchini with Garlic and Mint

Zucchine a Scapece

Makes 8 servings

Zucchini or other squash, eggplant, and carrots can be prepared a scapece, "in the style of Apicius," an early Roman who wrote about food. The vegetables are fried, flavored, and then chilled. Be sure to make this at least 24 hours before serving for best flavor.

2 pounds small zucchini

Vegetable oil for frying

3 tablespoons red wine vinegar

2 large garlic cloves, finely chopped

$\frac{1}{4}$ cup chopped fresh mint or basil

Salt and freshly ground black pepper

1. Scrub the zucchini with a brush under cold running water. Trim off the ends. Cut the zucchini into $^1/_4$-inch slices.

2. Pour 1 inch of oil into a deep heavy skillet or wide saucepan. Heat the oil over medium heat until a small piece of vegetable dropped into the oil sizzles.

3. Pat the zucchini slices dry with paper towels. Carefully slip about one-fourth of the zucchini into the hot oil. Cook until lightly browned around the edges, about 3 minutes. With a slotted spoon, transfer the zucchini to paper towels to drain. Fry the remainder in the same way.

4. Layer the zucchini in a dish, sprinkling each layer with some of the vinegar, garlic, mint, and salt and pepper to taste. Cover and refrigerate at least 24 hours before serving.

Sautéed Zucchini

Zucchine in Padella

Makes 6 servings

This is a quick way to make a tasty side dish with zucchini, onions, and parsley.

1 pound small zucchini

2 tablespoons unsalted butter

1 small onion, very finely chopped

Salt and freshly ground black pepper

3 tablespoons chopped flat-leaf parsley

1. Scrub the zucchini with a brush under cold running water. Trim off the ends. Cut into $^1/_8$-inch slices.

2. In a medium skillet over medium-low heat, melt the butter. Add the onion and cook until softened, about 5 minutes.

3. Add the zucchini and toss to coat with the butter. Cover and cook 5 minutes, or until the zucchini is just tender when pierced with a fork.

4. Add the salt and pepper to taste and parsley and toss well. Serve

immediately.

Zucchini with Prosciutto

Zucchine al Prosciutto

Makes 4 servings

These zucchini are good as a side dish with chicken, but also as a sauce for hot cooked penne or another pasta.

1½ pounds small zucchini

1 medium onion, chopped

2 tablespoons olive oil

1 garlic clove, chopped

½ teaspoon dried marjoram or thyme

Salt and freshly ground black pepper

3 thin slices imported Italian prosciutto, cut crosswise into narrow strips

1. Scrub the zucchini with a brush under cold running water. Trim off the ends. Cut the zucchini into 1/8-inch slices.

2. In a large skillet, cook the onion in the oil over medium heat. Cook, stirring, until the onion is tender and golden, about 10 minutes. Add the garlic and marjoram and cook 1 minute more.

3. Stir in the zucchini slices and salt and pepper to taste. Cook 5 minutes.

4. Add the prosciutto and cook until the zucchini are tender, about 2 minutes more. Serve hot.

Zucchini with Parmesan Crumbs

Zucchine alla Parmigiana

Makes 4 servings

Buttery, cheesy bread crumbs flavor this zucchini gratin.

1 pound small zucchini

2 tablespoons unsalted butter, melted and cooled

2 tablespoons bread crumbs, preferably homemade

¼ cup grated Parmigiano-Reggiano

Salt and freshly ground pepper

1. Scrub the zucchini with a brush under cold running water. Trim off the ends.

2. Place a rack in the center of the oven. Preheat oven to 425°F. Butter a 13 × 9 × 2–inch baking dish.

3. Spread the zucchini slices in the baking dish, overlapping slightly. In a medium bowl, mix together the butter, crumbs, cheese, and salt and pepper to taste. Sprinkle the crumb mixture over the zucchini.

4. Bake 30 minutes or until the crumbs are golden and the
zucchini are tender. Serve hot.

Zucchini Gratin

Zucchine Gratinate

Makes 4 to 6 servings

When I think of this gratin, I imagine serving it as part of a summer picnic buffet, with grilled meat or fish and several salads. It is good hot or cold.

2 medium yellow onions, chopped

2 garlic cloves, finely chopped

4 tablespoons olive oil

Salt and freshly ground black pepper

1 tablespoon chopped fresh thyme, basil, or oregano

4 small zucchini, cut into $\frac{1}{8}$-inch slices

3 medium round tomatoes, cut into thin slices

$\frac{1}{2}$ cup grated Parmigiano-Reggiano

1. In a medium skillet, cook the onions and garlic in 2 tablespoons of the olive oil over medium-low heat until golden, about 10 minutes. Season with salt and pepper to taste.

2. Place a rack in the center of the oven. Preheat the oven to 375°F. Oil a 13 × 9 × 2–inch baking dish.

3. Spread the onion mixture evenly in the baking dish. Scatter one-third of the thyme over the onions. Arrange the zucchini and tomatoes in overlapping slices over the onions. Sprinkle with the remaining thyme, and salt and pepper to taste. Drizzle with the remaining olive oil.

4. Bake 40 to 45 minutes or until the vegetables are tender and the juices are sizzling. Sprinkle with the cheese and bake until slighly melted, about 5 minutes more. Let rest 10 minutes before serving.

Zucchini with Tomatoes and Anchovies

Zucchine al Forno

Makes 4 servings

This southern-style gratin is flavored with anchovies and garlic.

1 pound small zucchini

4 plum tomatoes, thinly sliced

¼ cup plain dry bread crumbs

3 anchovy fillets, chopped

2 tablespoons olive oil

1 small garlic clove, finely chopped

Salt and freshly ground black pepper

1. Scrub the zucchini with a brush under cold running water. Trim off the ends. Cut into $1/8$-inch slices.

2. Place a rack in the center of the oven. Preheat the oven to 375°F. Oil a 13 × 9 × 2–inch baking pan. Arrange the zucchini and tomatoes in overlapping rows in the pan.

3. In a medium bowl, stir together the bread crumbs, anchovies, oil, garlic, and salt and pepper to taste. Scatter the mixture over the vegetables.

4. Bake 30 minutes, or until the vegetables are tender. Let rest 10 minutes before serving.

Zucchini Stew

Ciambotta di Zucchine

Makes 4 to 6 servings

Here is another member of the southern Italian ciambotta family of vegetable stews, one that my mom used to make again and again in the summer when I was growing up. Though I wasn't fond of it as a child, because we had it so often, I enjoy it—once in a while—now.

3 small to medium zucchini

2 medium onions, chopped

3 tablespoons olive oil

1 garlic clove, very finely chopped

4 plum tomatoes, cut into bite-size pieces

2 medium potatoes, peeled and cut into bite-size pieces

Salt and freshly ground black pepper

2 tablespoons chopped fresh basil

1. Scrub the zucchini with a brush under cold running water. Trim off the ends. Cut the zucchini into bite-size pieces.

2. In a large saucepan, cook the onions in the oil over medium heat until softened, about 5 minutes. Stir in the garlic and cook 1 minute more.

3. Add the tomatoes, zucchini, potatoes, and salt and pepper to taste. Cover and cook, stirring occasionally, 30 minutes or until the potatoes are very tender. Add a little water if the mixture seems dry.

4. When the ciambotta is done, remove from the heat and stir in the basil. Serve hot or at room temperature.

Savory Pie Pastry

Pasta Frolla Salata

Makes one 9- to 10-inch pie shell

A savory pie similar to a quiche can be made with cheese, eggs, and vegetables. These pies are good at room temperature or hot, and can be served as a piatto unico—one-dish meal—or as an appetizer. This pastry is good for all types of savory pies.

I roll out this dough between two sheets of plastic wrap. It prevents the dough from sticking to the board and rolling pin, so it is not necessary to add more flour, which can toughen the dough. To ensure that the crust is crisp on the bottom, I partially prebake the shell before adding the filling.

1½ cups all-purpose flour

1 teaspoon salt

½ cup (1 stick) unsalted butter, at room temperature

1 egg yolk

3 to 4 tablespoons ice water

1. Prepare the dough: Combine the flour and salt in a large bowl. With a pastry blender or a fork, cut in the butter until the mixture resembles coarse crumbs.

2. Beat the egg yolk together with 2 tablespoons of the water. Sprinkle the mixture over the flour. Mix together lightly until the dough is evenly moistened and comes together without being sticky. Add the remaining water if needed.

3. Shape the dough into a disk. Wrap in plastic wrap. Refrigerate 30 minutes or overnight.

4. If the dough has been refrigerated overnight, let it stand at room temperature 20 to 30 minutes before rolling it out. Place the dough between two sheets of plastic wrap and roll it out to a 12-inch circle, turning the dough and rearranging the plastic wrap with each turn. Remove the top sheet of plastic wrap. Using the remaining sheet to lift the dough, center the dough with the plastic up in a 9- to 10-inch tart pan with a removable base. Peel off the plastic wrap. Gently press the dough into the base and along the sides.

5. Roll the rolling pin over the top of the pan and trim off the overhanging dough. Press the dough against the side of the pan

to create a rim higher than the edge of the pan. Chill the pastry shell in the refrigerator 30 minutes.

6. Place the oven rack in the lower third of the oven. Preheat the oven to 450°F. With a fork, prick the bottom of the tart shell at 1-inch intervals. Bake for 5 minutes, then prick the dough again. Bake until just set, 10 minutes more. Remove the shell from the oven. Cool on a rack 10 minutes.

Spinach Ricotta Tart

Crostata di Spinaci

Makes 8 servings

I had a tart like this at Ferrara, a favorite restaurant in Rome. Something like a quiche, it is made with ricotta for extra creaminess. It is great for a lunch or brunch dish, served with a salad and chilled pinot grigio wine.

1 recipe Savory Pie Pastry

Filling

1 pound spinach, trimmed and rinsed

1/4 cup water

1 1/2 cups whole or part-skim ricotta

1/2 cup heavy cream

3/4 cup freshly grated Parmigiano-Reggiano

2 large eggs, beaten

1/4 teaspoon freshly grated nutmeg

Salt and freshly ground black pepper

1. Prepare and partially bake the crust. Reduce the oven temperature to 375°F.

2. Meanwhile, prepare the filling. Put the spinach in a large pot over medium heat with the water. Cover and cook 2 to 3 minutes or until wilted and tender. Drain and cool. Wrap the spinach in a lint-free cloth and squeeze out as much water as possible. Finely chop the spinach.

3. In a large bowl, beat together the spinach, ricotta, cream, cheese, eggs, nutmeg, and salt and pepper to taste. Scrape the mixture into the prepared tart shell.

4. Bake 35 to 40 minutes or until the filling is set and lightly browned.

5. Cool the tart in the pan 10 minutes. Remove the outer rim and place the tart on a serving dish. Serve warm or at room temperature.

Leek Tart

Crostata di Porri

Makes 6 to 8 servings

I had this tart at an enoteca, or wine bar, in Bologna. The nutty flavor of the Parmigiano and the cream enhance the sweet flavor of the leeks. It can also be made with sautéed mushrooms or peppers instead of the leeks.

1 recipe Savory Pie Pastry

Filling

4 medium leeks, about 1¼ pounds

3 tablespoons unsalted butter

Salt

2 large eggs

¾ cup heavy cream

⅓ cup freshly grated Parmigiano-Reggiano

Freshly grated nutmeg

Freshly ground black pepper

1. Prepare and partially bake the crust. Reduce the oven temperature to 375°F.

2. Prepare the filling: Trim off the roots and most of the green tops of the leeks. Cut them in half lengthwise and rinse them very well between each layer under cold running water. Cut the leeks into thin crosswise slices.

3. In a large skillet, melt the butter over medium heat. Add the leeks and a pinch of salt. Cook, stirring often, until the leeks are tender when pierced with a knife, about 20 minutes. Remove the pan from the heat and let cool.

4. In a medium bowl, beat together the eggs, cream, cheese, and a pinch of nutmeg. Stir in the leeks and pepper to taste.

5. Scrape the mixture into the partially baked tart shell. Bake 35 to 40 minutes or until the filling is set. Serve warm or at room temperature.

Mozzarella, Basil, and Roasted Pepper Sandwiches

Panini di Mozzarella

Makes 2 servings

I sometimes make this sandwich substituting arugula for the basil and prosciutto for the red peppers.

4 ounces fresh mozzarella cheese, cut into 8 slices

4 slices country bread

4 fresh basil leaves

$\frac{1}{4}$ cup roasted red or yellow bell peppers, cut into thin strips

1. Trim the mozzarella slices to fit the bread. If the mozzarella is juicy, pat it dry. Lay half the cheese in a single layer on two slices of bread.

2. Arrange the basil leaves and peppers on the cheese and top with the remaining mozzarella. Place the remaining bread on top and press down firmly with your hands.

3. Preheat a sandwich press or stove-top grill pan. Place the sandwiches in the press and cook until toasted, about 4 to 5

minutes. If using a grill pan, place a heavy weight such as a frying pan on top. Turn the sandwiches when browned on one side, cover with the weight, and toast on the second side. Serve hot.

Spinach and Robiola Sandwiches

Panino di Spinaci e Robiola

Makes 2 servings

Focaccia adds nice flavor and texture to pressed panini. Other greens can be substituted for the spinach, or use leftover vegetables. For the cheese, I like to use robiola, a soft creamy cheese made from cow's, goat's, or sheep's milk, or a combination, from Piedmont and Lombardy. Other possibilities are fresh goat cheese or even whipped cream cheese. Add a drop or two of truffle oil to the filling for an earthy flavor and a touch of luxury.

1 (10-ounce) package fresh spinach

4 ounces fresh robiola, or substitute goat cheese

Truffle oil (optional)

2 serving-size squares or wedges of fresh focaccia

1. Put the spinach in a large pot over medium heat with $^1/_4$ cup of water. Cover and cook 2 to 3 minutes or until wilted and tender. Drain and cool. Wrap the spinach in a lint-free cloth and squeeze out as much water as possible.

2. Finely chop the spinach and place it in a medium bowl. Add the cheese and mash the spinach into the cheese. Add a drop or two of truffle oil, if you like.

3. With a long serrated knife, carefully cut the focaccia in half horizontally. Spread the mixture on the inside of the bottom halves of the focaccia. Place the tops on the sandwiches and flatten gently.

4. Preheat a sandwich press or stove-top grill pan. If using a press, place the sandwiches in the press and cook until toasted, about 4 to 5 minutes. If using a grill pan, place the sandwiches on the pan, then a heavy weight, such as a frying pan, on top.

5. When browned on one side, turn the sandwiches, cover with the weight, and toast on the second side. Serve hot.

Riviera Sandwich

Panino della Riviera

Makes 4 servings

The geographic border dividing Italy and France does not also signify a distinction in the food eaten on either side. With their similar climate and geography, people living along the Italian and French coasts share very similar food customs. A case in point is the French pan bagnat and Italian pane bagnato, meaning "bathed bread," which is sometimes called a Riviera sandwich in Italy. This hearty sandwich, bathed in a lively vinaigrette dressing, is stuffed with tuna and roasted peppers in France. On the Italian side of the border, mozzarella stands in for the tuna, and anchovies are added, but the rest is pretty much the same. This is the perfect sandwich to take on a picnic, because the flavors marry well, and it only gets better as it stands.

1 loaf Italian bread, about 12 inches long

Dressing

1 garlic clove, very finely chopped

¼ cup olive oil

2 tablespoons vinegar

$1/2$ teaspoon dried oregano, crumbled

Salt and freshly ground black pepper

2 ripe tomatoes, sliced

1 (2-ounce) can anchovies

8 ounces sliced mozzarella

2 peeled and seeded roasted peppers with their juice

12 oil-cured olives, pitted and chopped

1. Cut the bread loaf in half lengthwise and remove the soft bread inside.

2. In a small bowl, whisk together the dressing ingredients and pour half the dressing over the cut sides of the bread. Layer the bottom half of the bread with the tomatoes, anchovies, mozzarella, roasted peppers, and olives, drizzling each layer with some of the dressing.

3. Place the top on the sandwich and press it together. Wrap in foil and cover with a board or heavy pan. Let stand at room temperature up to 2 hours or store in the refrigerator overnight.

4. Slice into 3-inch-wide sandwiches. Serve at room temperature.

Tuna and Roasted Pepper Triangle Sandwiches

Tramezzini al Tonno e Peperoni

Makes 3 sandwiches

Some of the same flavors of the hearty Riviera sandwich find their way into this delicate triangle sandwich I tasted at a favorite Roman café. The tuna was seasoned with fennel seeds, but I like to substitute fennel pollen, which is nothing more than ground-up fennel seeds, but has more flavor. A lot of chefs are using it these days, and it can be found in gourmet shops specializing in dried herbs as well as on Internet sites. If you can't find fennel pollen, substitute fennel seeds, which you can grind yourself in a spice grinder or chop with a knife.

1 small roasted red pepper, drained and cut into thin strips

Extra-virgin olive oil

Salt

1 (3½-ounce) can Italian tuna packed in olive oil

2 tablespoons mayonnaise

1 to 2 teaspoons fresh lemon juice

1 tablespoon chopped green onion

1 teaspoon fennel pollen

4 slices good-quality white sandwich bread

1. Toss the roasted pepper with a little oil and salt.

2. Drain the tuna and place it in a bowl. Mash the tuna well with a fork. Blend in the mayonnaise, lemon juice to taste, and green onion.

3. Spread the tuna on two of the bread slices. Top with the pepper strips. Cover with the remaining bread, pressing down slightly.

4. With a large chef's knife, trim off the bread crusts. Cut the sandwiches in half diagonally to form two triangles. Serve immediately or cover tightly with plastic wrap and refrigerate until ready to serve.

Prosciutto and Fig Triangle Sandwiches

Tramezzini di Prosciutto e Fichi

Makes 2 sandwiches

The saltiness of the prosciutto and sweetness of the fig jam offer a pleasant contrast in this sandwich. It is very good as an appetizer if you cut it into quarters. Serve it with sparkling Prosecco.

Unsalted butter, at room temperature

4 slices good-quality white sandwich bread

About 2 tablespoons fig jam

4 thin slices imported Italian prosciutto

1. Spread a little butter on one side of each slice of bread. Spread about 2 teaspoons fig jam over the butter on each slice.

2. Arrange two slices of prosciutto on half of the slices. Place the remaining slices of bread jam-side-down on the prosciutto.

3. With a large chef's knife, trim off the bread crusts. Cut the sandwiches in half diagonally to form two triangles. Serve immediately or cover with plastic wrap and refrigerate.

Amaretto Baked Apples

Mele al'Amaretto

Makes 6 servings

Amaretto is a sweet liqueur; amaretti are crisp cookies. Both of these Italian products are flavored with two kinds of almonds—the familiar variety, plus a slightly bitter almond that is not eaten on its own, though it is frequently used in Italy to flavor desserts. Amaro means "bitter," and both the liqueur and the cookies take their name from these almonds. Both are widely available—the cookies in specialty shops and by mail order and the liqueur in many liquor stores.

The most familiar brand of amaretti cookies is packaged in distinctive red tins or boxes. The cookies are wrapped in pairs in pastel tissue paper. There are other brands of amaretti that pack the cookies loose in bags. I always have amaretti in the house. They keep a long time and are nice with a cup of tea, or as an ingredient in a number of sweet and savory dishes.

Golden delicious are the apples I prefer for baking. The locally grown ones are sweet and crisp, yet they hold their shape nicely when baked.

6 baking apples, such as golden delicious

6 amaretti cookies

6 tablespoons sugar

2 tablespoons unsalted butter

6 tablespoons amaretto or rum

1. Place a rack in the center of the oven. Preheat the oven to 375°F. Butter a baking dish just large enough to hold the apples standing upright.

2. Remove the apple cores and peel the apples about two-thirds of the way down from the stem end.

3. Place the amaretti cookies in a plastic bag and crush them gently with a heavy object, such as a rolling pin. In a medium bowl, blend the crumbs with the sugar and butter.

4. Stuff a little of the mixture into the center of each apple. Spoon the amaretto over the apples. Pour 1 cup water around the apples.

5. Bake 45 minutes or until the apples are tender when pierced with a knife. Serve warm or at room temperature.

Livia's Apple Cake

Torta di Mele alla Livia

Makes 8 servings

My friend Livia Colantonio lives in Umbria on a farm called Podernovo. The farm raises Chianina cattle, grows a variety of wine grapes, and bottles wine under the Castello delle Regine label.

Guests can stay in one of the beautifully restored guesthouses at Podernovo, which is just 45 minutes from Rome, and enjoy a restful vacation. Livia makes this simple but sensational "cake" that is always good after a fall or winter meal. It isn't a cake in the traditional sense, because it is made almost entirely of apples, with just a few cookie crumbs between the layers to hold some of the fruit juices. Serve it with a dollop of whipped cream or rum-raisin ice cream.

You will need a round pan or baking dish 9 inches wide by 3 inches deep. Use a cake pan, or a casserole or soufflé dish, but do not use a springform pan because the apple juices will leak out.

12 amaretti cookies

3 pounds golden delicious, Granny Smith, or other firm apples (about 6 large)

½ cup sugar

1. Place the amaretti cookies in a plastic bag and crush them gently with a heavy object, such as a rolling pin. You should have about $3/4$ cup of crumbs.

2. Peel the apples and cut them into quarters lengthwise. Cut the quarters into $1/8$-inch-thick slices.

3. Place a rack in the center of the oven. Preheat the oven to 350°F. Generously butter a 9 × 3–inch round baking pan or a tube pan. Line the bottom of the pan with a circle of parchment paper. Butter the paper.

4. Make a layer of apples overlapping slightly in the bottom of the pan. Sprinkle with a little of the crumbs and sugar. Alternate layers of the remaining apple slices in the pan with the remaining crumbs and sugar. The apple slices do not have to be arranged neatly. Place a sheet of foil over the top, molding it over the rim of the pan.

5. Bake the apples $1^1/2$ hours. Uncover and bake 30 minutes more or until the apples are tender when pierced with a knife and

diminished in volume. Transfer the pan to a wire rack. Let cool at least 15 minutes. Run a knife around the edge of the pan. Holding the pan with a pot holder in one hand, place a flat serving plate over the top of the pan. Invert them both, so the apples transfer onto the plate.

6. Serve at room temperature, cut into wedges. Cover with an inverted bowl and store in the refrigerator up to 3 days.

Apricots in Lemon Syrup

Albicocche al Limone

Makes 6 servings

Perfectly ripe apricots really need no enhancement, but if you have some that are less than perfect, try cooking them in a simple lemon syrup. Serve the poached apricots chilled, possibly with amaretto-flavored whipped cream.

1 cup cold water

¼ cup sugar, or to taste

2 (2-inch) strips lemon zest

2 tablespoons fresh lemon juice

1 pound apricots (about 8)

1. In a saucepan or skillet large enough to hold the apricot halves in a single layer, combine the water, sugar, zest, and juice. Bring to a simmer over medium-low heat and cook, swirling the pan once or twice, for 10 minutes.

2. Following the line on the apricots, cut them in half and remove the pits. Place the halves in the simmering syrup. Cook, turning once, until the fruit is tender, about 5 minutes.

3. Let the apricots cool briefly in the syrup, then cover and store in the refrigerator. Serve chilled.

Berries with Lemon and Sugar

Frutti di Bosco al Limone

Makes 4 servings

Fresh lemon juice and sugar bring out all the flavor of berries. Try this with just one berry variety or a combination. Top the dressed berries with a scoop of lemon ice or sorbet if you like.

One of my favorite berries, the tiny wild strawberry (fragoline del bosco), is common in Italy but not widely available here. Wild strawberries have a mouthwatering strawberry aroma and are easy to grow in a flowerpot. Seeds are available from many catalog companies, and you can buy the plants at many nurseries here in the United States.

1 cup sliced strawberries

1 cup blackberries

1 cup blueberries

1 cup raspberries

Freshly squeezed lemon juice (about 2 tablespoons)

Sugar (about 1 tablespoon)

1. In a large bowl, gently toss the berries together. Drizzle with the lemon juice and sugar to taste. Taste and adjust seasoning.

2. Place the berries in shallow serving dishes. Serve immediately.

Strawberries with Balsamic Vinegar

Fragole al Balsamico

Makes 2 servings

If you can find the little wild strawberries known in Italian as fragoline del bosco, use them in this dessert. But ordinary fresh strawberries, too, will benefit from a quick marinate in aged balsamic vinegar. Like a sprinkle of fresh lemon juice on a piece of fish, or salt on a steak, the intense sweet-and-tangy flavor of balsamic vinegar enhances many foods. Think of it as a condiment rather than as a vinegar.

You probably will have to buy aged balsamic vinegar at a specialty store. In the New York area, one of my favorite sources is Di Palo Fine Foods on Grand Street in Little Italy (see Sources). Louis Di Palo is a walking encyclopedia on balsamic vinegar, as well as just about any other food product imported from Italy. The first time I asked for balsamico, he brought out several bottles and offered everyone in the shop samples as he explained each one.

The best balsamico is made in the provinces of Modena and Reggio in Emilia-Romagna. Smooth, complex, and syrupy, it tastes more like a rich liqueur than a harsh vinegar, and it is often drunk as a cordial.

Look for the words Aceto Balsamico Tradizionale on the label.

Though it is expensive, a little bit goes a long way.

1 pint wild or cultivated strawberries, sliced if large

2 tablespoons best-quality aged balsamic vinegar, or to taste

2 tablespoons sugar

In a medium bowl, toss the strawberries with the vinegar and sugar. Let stand 15 minutes before serving.

Raspberries with Mascarpone and Balsamic Vinegar

Lampone con Mascarpone e Balsamico

Makes 4 servings

Always rinse delicate raspberries just before you are ready to use them—if you rinse them earlier, the moisture could cause them to spoil more quickly. Before serving them, look them over and discard those that show any signs of mold. Store berries in an uncovered shallow container in the refrigerator, but use them as soon as possible after purchasing them, as they deteriorate rapidly.

Mascarpone is a thick, smooth cream that is called a cheese, though it has only the slightest cheesy tang. It has a texture similar to sour cream, or slightly thicker. If you prefer, crème fraîche, ricotta, or sour cream can be substituted.

1½ cups mascarpone

About ¼ cup sugar

1 to 2 tablespoons best-quality aged balsamic vinegar

2 cups raspberries, lightly rinsed and dried

1. In a small bowl, whisk the mascarpone and sugar until well
blended. Stir in the balsamic vinegar to taste. Let stand 15
minutes and stir again.

2. Divide the raspberries among 4 goblets or serving bowls. Top
with the mascarpone and serve immediately.

Cherries in Barolo

Ciliege al Barolo

Makes 4 servings

Here, sweet, ripe cherries are simmered Piedmont style in Barolo or another full-bodied red wine.

¾ cup sugar

1 cup Barolo or other dry red wine

1 pound ripe sweet cherries, pitted

1 cup heavy or whipping cream, well chilled

1. At least 20 minutes before you are ready to whip the cream, place a large bowl and the beaters of an electric mixer in the refrigerator.

2. In a large saucepan, combine the sugar and wine. Bring to a simmer and cook 5 minutes.

3. Add the cherries. After the liquid returns to a simmer, cook until the cherries are tender when pierced with a knife, about 10 minutes more. Let cool.

4. Just before serving, remove the bowl and beaters from the refrigerator. Pour the cream into the bowl and whip the cream at high speed until it holds its shape softly when the beaters are lifted, about 4 minutes.

5. Spoon the cherries into serving bowls. Serve at room temperature or slightly chilled with whipped cream.

Hot Roasted Chestnuts

Caldarroste

Makes 8 servings

St. Martin's Day, November 11, is celebrated all over Italy with hot roasted chestnuts and newly made red wine. The celebration marks not only the feast day of a beloved saint who was known for his kindness to the poor, but also the end of the growing season, the day the earth goes into repose for winter.

Roasted chestnuts are also a classic finishing touch to winter holiday meals throughout Italy. I put them in the oven to cook when we sit down to dinner, and by the time we are finished with our main course, they are ready to eat.

1 pound fresh chestnuts

1. Place a rack in the center of the oven. Preheat the oven to 425°F. Rinse the chestnuts and pat them dry. Place the chestnuts flat-side down on a cutting board. Carefully cut an X on the top of each with the tip of a small sharp knife.

2. Place the chestnuts on a large sheet of heavy-duty aluminum foil. Fold one end over the other to enclose the chestnuts. Fold

the ends over to seal. Place the package in a baking pan. Roast the chestnuts until tender when pierced with a small knife, about 45 to 60 minutes.

3. Transfer the foil package to a cooling rack. Leave the chestnuts wrapped in the foil for 10 minutes. Serve hot.

Fig Preserves

Marmellata di Fichi

Makes 1½ pints

Fig trees, both domesticated and wild, grow all over Italy, except in the northernmost regions where it is too cold. Because they are so sweet and widely available, figs are used in many desserts, especially in southern Italy. Ripe figs do not keep well, so when they are abundant in late summer they are preserved in several different ways. In Puglia, the figs are cooked with water to make thick, sweet syrup that is used for desserts. Figs are also dried in the sun or turned into fig preserves.

A small batch of fig preserves is easy to make and can be stored for a month in the refrigerator. For longer storage, the jam should be canned (following safe canning methods) or frozen. Serve it as a complement to a cheese course or for breakfast on buttered walnut bread.

1½ pounds fresh ripe figs, rinsed and dried

2 cups sugar

2 strips lemon zest

1. Peel the figs and cut them into quarters. Place them in a medium bowl with sugar and lemon zest. Stir well. Cover and refrigerate overnight.

2. The next day, transfer the contents of the bowl to a large heavy saucepan. Bring to a simmer over medium heat. Cook, stirring occasionally, until the mixture thickens slightly, about 5 minutes. To test if the mixture is thick enough, place a drop of the slightly cooled liquid between your thumb and index finger. If the mixture forms a thread when the thumb and finger are slightly separated, the preserves are ready.

3. Spoon into sterilized jars and store in the refrigerator up to 30 days.

Chocolate-Dipped Figs

Fichi al Cioccolato

Makes 8 to 10 servings

Moist dried figs stuffed with nuts and dipped in chocolate are nice as a little after-dinner treat.

I like to buy candied orange peel at Kalustyan's, a shop in New York City that specializes in spices, dried fruits, and nuts. Because they sell a lot of it, it is always fresh and full of flavor. Many other specialty shops sell good candied orange peel. You can also order it by mail (see Sources). Supermarket candied orange peel and other fruits are chopped into small bits and usually dry and tasteless.

18 moist dried figs (about 1 pound)

18 toasted almonds

½ cup candied orange peel

4 ounces bittersweet chocolate, chopped or broken into small pieces

2 tablespoons unsalted butter

1. Line a tray with wax paper and set a wire cooling rack on top. Make a small slit in the base of each fig. Insert an almond and a piece of orange peel into the figs. Pinch the slit closed.

2. In the top half of a double boiler set over simmering water, melt the chocolate and butter, about 5 minutes. Remove from the heat and stir until smooth. Let stand 5 minutes.

3. Dip each fig in the melted chocolate and place on the wire rack. When all of the figs have been dipped, place the tray in the refrigerator to set the chocolate, about 1 hour.

4. Place the figs in an airtight container, separating each layer with wax paper. Store in the refrigerator up to 30 days.

Figs in Wine Syrup

Fichi alla Contadina

Makes 8 servings

Dried calimyrna and mission figs from California are moist and plump. Either variety can be used for this recipe. After poaching, they are good as is, or served with ice cream or whipped cream. They also go well with gorgonzola cheese.

1 cup vin santo, Marsala, or dry red wine

2 tablespoons honey

2 (2-inch) strips lemon zest

18 moist dried figs (about 1 pound)

1. In a medium saucepan, combine the vin santo, honey, and lemon zest. Bring to a simmer over low heat and cook 1 minute.

2. Add the figs and cold water to cover. Bring the liquid to a simmer over low heat and cover the pot. Cook until the figs are tender, about 10 minutes.

3. With a slotted spoon, transfer the figs from the pot to a bowl. Cook the liquid, uncovered, until reduced and slightly thickened, about 5 minutes. Pour the syrup over the figs and let cool. Refrigerate at least 1 hour and up to 3 days. Serve slightly chilled.

Dora's Baked Figs

Fichi al Forno

Makes 2 dozen

Dried figs stuffed with nuts are a Pugliese specialty. This recipe is from my friend Dora Marzovilla, who serves them as an after-dinner treat at her family's New York restaurant, I Trulli. Serve the figs with a glass of dessert wine, such as Moscato di Pantelleria.

24 moist dried figs (about 1½ pounds), stem ends removed

24 toasted almonds

1 tablespoon fennel seeds

¼ cup bay leaves

1. Place a rack in the center of the oven. Preheat the oven to 350°F. Remove the hard stem ends from each fig. With a small knife, cut a slit in the base of the figs. Insert an almond in the figs and pinch the slit closed.

2. Arrange the figs on a baking sheet and bake 15 to 20 minutes or until lightly browned. Let cool on a wire rack.

3. Make a layer of the figs in a 1-quart airtight plastic or glass container. Sprinkle with some of the fennel seeds. Top with a layer of bay leaves. Repeat the layering until all of the ingredients are used. Cover and store in a cool place (but not the refrigerator) at least 1 week before serving.

Honeydew in Mint Syrup

Melone alla Menta

Makes 4 servings

After a big fish dinner at a seaside restaurant in Sicily, we were served this cool combination of honeydew melon bathed in a fresh mint syrup.

1 cup cold water

½ cup sugar

½ cup packed fresh spearmint leaves, plus more for garnish

8 to 12 slices peeled ripe honeydew melon

1. In a saucepan, combine the water, sugar, and mint leaves. Bring to a simmer and cook 1 minute or until the leaves are wilted. Remove from the heat. Let cool, then pass the syrup through a fine-mesh strainer into a bowl to strain out the mint leaves.

2. Place the melon on a serving platter and pour the syrup over the melon. Chill in the refrigerator briefly. Serve garnished with mint leaves.

Oranges in Orange Syrup

Arancia Marinate

Makes 8 servings

Juicy oranges in a sweet syrup are a perfect dessert after a rich meal. I especially like to serve these in winter when fresh oranges are at their best. Arranged on a platter, the oranges look very pretty with their topping of orange zest strips and glistening syrup. As a variation, cut the oranges into wedges and combine them with sliced ripe pineapple. Serve the orange sauce over all.

8 large navel oranges

1¼ cups sugar

2 tablespoons orange brandy or liqueur

1. Scrub the oranges with a brush. Trim off the ends. With a vegetable peeler, peel off the colored part of the orange skin (the zest) in wide strips. Avoid digging into the bitter white pith. Stack the zest strips and cut them into narrow matchstick pieces.

2. Remove the white pith from the oranges. Place the oranges on a serving platter.

3. Bring a small saucepan of water to a boil. Add the orange zest and bring to a simmer. Cook 1 minute. Drain the zest and rinse under cool water. Repeat. (This will help to remove some of the bitterness from the zest.)

4. Place the sugar and $1/4$ cup of water in another small saucepan over medium heat. Bring the mixture to a boil. Cook until the sugar is melted and the syrup thickens, about 3 minutes. Stir in the orange zest and cook 3 minutes more. Let cool.

5. Add the orange brandy to the contents of the pot. With a fork, remove the orange zest from the syrup and pile it on top of the oranges. Spoon on the syrup. Cover and chill up to 3 hours until ready to serve.

Oranges Gratinéed with Zabaglione

Arancia allo Zabaglione

Makes 4 servings

Gratiné is a French word meaning to brown the surface of a dish. Usually it applies to savory foods that are sprinkled with bread crumbs or cheese to help them brown.

Zabaglione is typically served plain or as a sauce for fruit or cake. Here it is spooned over oranges and broiled briefly until it browns slightly and forms a creamy topping. Bananas, kiwis, berries, or other soft fruits can also be prepared this way.

6 navel oranges, peeled and thinly sliced

Zabaglione

1 large egg

2 large egg yolks

⅓ cup sugar

⅓ cup dry or sweet Marsala

1. Preheat the broiler. Arrange the orange slices in a flameproof baking dish, overlapping slightly.

2. Prepare the zabaglione: Fill a small saucepan or the bottom of a double boiler with 2 inches of water. Bring it to a simmer over low heat. In a bowl larger than the rim of the pan or the top of the double boiler, combine the egg, yolks, sugar, and Marsala. Beat with a hand-held electric beater until foamy. Place over the pan of simmering water. Beat until the mixture is pale-colored and holds a soft shape when the beaters are lifted, about 5 minutes.

3. Spread the zabaglione over the oranges. Put the dish under the broiler 1 to 2 minutes or until the zabaglione is browned in spots. Serve immediately.

White Peaches in Asti Spumante

Pesche Bianche in Asti Spumante

Makes 4 servings

Asti Spumante is a sweet, sparkling dessert wine from Piedmont in northwestern Italy. It has a delicate orange-blossom flavor and aroma that comes from muscat grapes. If you can't find white peaches, yellow peaches will work well or substitute another summer fruit, such as nectarines, plums, or apricots.

4 large ripe white peaches

1 tablespoon sugar

8 ounces chilled Asti Spumante

1. Peel and pit the peaches. Cut them into thin slices.

2. Toss the peaches with the sugar and let stand 10 minutes.

3. Spoon the peaches into goblets or parfait glasses. Pour on the Asti Spumante and serve immediately.

Peaches in Red Wine

Pesche al Vino Rosso

Makes 4 servings

I remember watching my grandfather cutting up his homegrown white peaches to soak in a pitcher of red wine. The sweet peach juices tamed any roughness in the wine. White peaches are my favorite, but yellow peaches or nectarines are good too.

$\frac{1}{3}$ cup sugar, or to taste

2 cups fruity red wine

4 ripe peaches

1. In a medium bowl, combine the sugar and wine.

2. Cut the peaches in half and remove the pits. Cut the peaches into bite-size pieces. Stir them into the wine. Cover and refrigerate 2 to 3 hours.

3. Spoon the peaches and wine into goblets and serve.

Amaretti-Stuffed Peaches

Pesche al Forno

Makes 4 servings

This is a favorite dessert from Piedmont. Serve it drizzled with heavy cream or topped with a scoop of ice cream.

8 medium peaches, not too ripe

8 amaretti cookies

2 tablespoons softened unsalted butter

2 tablespoons sugar

1 large egg

1. Place a rack in the center of the oven. Preheat the oven to 375°F. Butter a baking dish large enough to hold the peach halves in a single layer.

2. Place the amaretti cookies in a plastic bag and crush them gently with a heavy object, such as a rolling pin. You should have about $^1/_2$ cup. In a medium bowl, mix together the butter and sugar and stir in the crumbs.

3. Following the line around the peaches, cut them in half and remove the pits. With a grapefruit spoon or a melon baller, scoop out a little of the peach flesh from the center to widen the opening and add it to the crumb mixture. Stir the egg into the mixture.

4. Arrange the peach halves cut sides up in the dish. Spoon some of the crumb mixture into each peach half.

5. Bake 1 hour or until the peaches are tender. Serve hot or at room temperature.

Pears in Orange Sauce

Pere all' Arancia

Makes 4 servings

When I visited Anna Tasca Lanza at Regaleali, her family's wine estate in Sicily, she gave me some of her excellent mandarin orange marmalade to take home. Anna uses the marmalade both as a spread and as a dessert sauce, and inspired me to stir some into the poaching liquid of some pears I was cooking. The pears had a beautiful golden glaze, and everyone loved the result. Now I make this dessert often. Because I quickly used up the supply of marmalade Anna gave me, I use quality store-bought orange marmalade.

½ cup sugar

1 cup dry white wine

4 firm ripe pears, such as Anjou, Bartlett, or Bosc

⅓ cup orange marmalade

2 tablespoons orange liqueur or rum

1. In a saucepan just large enough to hold the pears upright, combine the sugar and wine. Over medium heat, bring to a simmer and cook until the sugar is dissolved.

2. Add the pears. Cover the pan and cook about 30 minutes or until the pears are tender when pierced with a knife.

3. With a slotted spoon, transfer the pears to a serving platter. Add the marmalade to the liquid in the saucepan. Bring to a simmer and cook 1 minute. Remove from the heat and stir in the liqueur. Spoon the sauce over and around the pears. Cover and chill in the refrigerator at least 1 hour before serving.

Pears with Marsala and Cream

Pere al Marsala

Makes 4 servings

I had pears prepared this way at a trattoria in Bologna. If you prepare them just before eating dinner, they will be at the right serving temperature when you are ready for dessert.

You can find both dry and sweet Marsala imported from Sicily, though the dry is of better quality. Either can be used for making desserts.

4 large Anjou, Bartlett, or Bosc pears, not too ripe

¼ cup sugar

½ cup water

½ cup dry or sweet Marsala

¼ cup heavy cream

1. Peel the pears and cut them in half lengthwise.

2. In a skillet large enough to hold the pear halves in a single layer, bring the sugar and water to a simmer over medium heat. Stir to dissolve the sugar. Add the pears and cover the skillet. Cook 5 to 10 minutes or until the pears are almost tender when pierced with a fork.

3. With a slotted spoon, transfer the pears to a plate. Add the Marsala to the skillet and bring to a simmer. Cook until the syrup is slightly thickened, about 5 minutes. Stir in the cream and simmer 2 minutes more.

4. Return the pears to the skillet and baste them with the sauce. Transfer the pears to serving dishes and spoon the sauce over the top. Let cool to room temperature before serving.

Pears with Warm Chocolate Sauce

Pere Affogato al Cioccolato

Makes 6 servings

Sweet fresh pears bathed in a bittersweet chocolate sauce is a classic European dessert. I had this in Bologna, where the chocolate sauce was made with Majani chocolate, a locally made brand that unfortunately does not travel far from its hometown. Use a good-quality bittersweet chocolate. One brand that I like, Scharffen Berger, is made in California.

6 Anjou, Bartlett, or Bosc pears, not too ripe

2 cups water

3/4 cup sugar

4 (2 × 1/2–inch) strips orange zest, cut into matchsticks

1 1/2 cups Warm Chocolate Sauce

1. Peel the pears, leaving the stems intact. With a melon baller or small spoon, scoop out the core and seeds, working from the bottom of the pears.

2. In a saucepan large enough to hold all the pears upright, bring the water, sugar, and orange zest to a simmer over medium heat. Stir until the sugar is dissolved.

3. Add the pears and reduce the heat to low. Cover the pan and cook, turning the pears once, for 20 minutes or until tender when pierced with a small knife. Let the pears cool in the syrup.

4. When ready to serve, prepare the chocolate sauce.

5. With a slotted spoon, transfer the pears to serving dishes. (Cover and refrigerate the syrup for another use, such as tossing with cut-up fruits for a salad.) Drizzle with warm chocolate sauce. Serve immediately.

Rum-Spiced Pears

Pere al Rhum

Makes 6 servings

The sweet, mild, almost floral taste of ripe pears lends itself to many other complementary flavors. Fruits such as oranges, lemons, and berries and many cheeses go well with them, and Marsala and dry wines are often used to poach pears. In Piedmont I was pleasantly surprised to be served these pears simmered in a spiced rum syrup accompanying a simple hazelnut cake.

6 Anjou, Bartlett, or Bosc pears, not too ripe

¼ cup brown sugar

¼ cup dark rum

¼ cup water

4 whole cloves

1. Peel the pears, leaving the stems intact. With a melon baller or small spoon, scoop out the core and seeds, working from the bottom of the pears.

2. In a saucepan just large enough to hold the pears, stir together the sugar, rum, and water over medium heat until the sugar is melted, about 5 minutes. Add the pears. Scatter the cloves around the fruit.

3. Cover the pan and bring the liquid to a simmer. Cook over medium-low heat 15 to 20 minutes or until the pears are tender when pierced with a knife. With a slotted spoon, transfer the pears to a serving dish.

4. Simmer the liquid uncovered until reduced and syrupy. Strain the liquid over the pears. Let cool.

5. Serve at room temperature or cover and chill in the refrigerator.

Spiced Pears with Pecorino

Pere allo Spezie e Pecorino

Makes 6 servings

Tuscans are rightly proud of their excellent sheep's milk cheese. Every town has its own version, and each tastes slightly different from the others, depending on how it is aged and where the milk comes from. Usually the cheeses are eaten when they are quite young and still semifirm. When eaten for dessert, the cheese is sometimes drizzled with a little honey or served with pears. I like this sophisticated presentation that I had in Montalcino—pecorino served with pears cooked in the local red wine and spices, accompanied by fresh walnuts.

Of course, the pears are also good served plain or with a large spoonful of whipped cream.

6 medium Anjou, Bartlett, or Bosc pears, not too ripe

1 cup dry red wine

½ cup sugar

1 (3-inch) piece cinnamon stick

4 whole cloves

8 ounces Pecorino Toscano, Asiago, or Parmigiano-Reggiano cheese, cut into 6 pieces

12 walnut halves, toasted

1. Place a rack in the center of the oven. Preheat the oven to 450°F. Arrange the pears in a baking dish just large enough to hold them upright.

2. Stir together the wine and sugar until the sugar softens. Pour the mixture over the pears. Scatter the cinnamon and cloves around the pears.

3. Bake the pears, basting them occasionally with the wine, 45 to 60 minutes or until they are tender when pierced with a knife. If the liquid begins to dry up before the pears are done, add a little warm water to the pan.

4. Let the pears cool in the dish, basting them occasionally with the pan juices. (As the juices cool, they thicken and coat the pears with a rich red glaze.) Remove the spices.

5. Serve the pears with the syrup at room temperature or slightly chilled. Place them on serving dishes with two walnut halves and a piece of the cheese.

Poached Pears with Gorgonzola

Pere al Gorgonzola

Makes 4 servings

The spicy flavor of gorgonzola cheese blended to a smooth cream is a savory complement to these pears poached in a lemony white-wine syrup. A sprinkling of pistachios adds a bright touch of color. Anjou, Bartlett, and Bosc pears are my favorite varieties for poaching, because their slender shape allows them to cook through evenly. Poached pears hold their shape better when the fruit are not too ripe.

2 cups dry white wine

2 tablespoons fresh lemon juice

¾ cup sugar

2 (2-inch) strips lemon zest

4 pears, such as Anjou, Bartlett, or Bosc

4 ounces gorgonzola

2 tablespoons ricotta, mascarpone, or heavy cream

2 tablespoons chopped pistachios

1. In a medium saucepan, combine the wine, lemon juice, sugar, and lemon zest. Bring to a simmer and cook for 10 minutes.

2. Meanwhile, peel the pears and cut them in half lengthwise. Remove the cores.

3. Slip the pears into the wine syrup and cook until tender when pierced with a knife, about 10 minutes. Let cool.

4. With a slotted spoon, transfer two pear halves to each serving dish, cored-side up. Drizzle the syrup around the pears.

5. In a small bowl, mash the gorgonzola with the ricotta to make a smooth paste. Scoop some of the cheese mixture into the cored space of each pear half. Sprinkle with the pistachios. Serve immediately.

Pear or Apple Pudding Cake

Budino di Pere o Mele

Makes 6 servings

Not quite a cake or a pudding, this dessert consists of fruit cooked until tender, then baked with a slightly cakelike topping. It is good with apples or pears or even peaches or plums.

I like to use dark rum for flavoring this dessert, but light rum, cognac, or even grappa can be substituted.

¾ cup raisins

½ cup dark rum, cognac, or grappa

2 tablespoons unsalted butter

8 firm ripe pears or apples, peeled and cut into ½-inch slices

⅓ cup sugar

Topping

6 tablespoons unsalted butter, melted and cooled

⅓ cup sugar

½ cup all-purpose flour

3 large eggs, separated

⅔ cup whole milk

2 tablespoons dark rum, cognac, or grappa

1 teaspoon pure vanilla extract

Pinch of salt

Confectioner's sugar

1. In a small bowl, toss together the raisins and rum. Let stand for 30 minutes.

2. Melt the butter in a large skillet over medium heat. Add the fruit and sugar. Cook, stirring occasionally, until the fruit is almost tender, about 7 minutes. Add the raisins and rum. Cook 2 minutes more. Remove from the heat.

3. Place a rack in the center of the oven. Preheat the oven to 350°F. Grease a 13 × 9 × 2–inch baking dish. Spoon the fruit mixture into the baking dish.

4. Prepare the topping: In a large bowl, with an electric mixer, beat the butter and sugar until blended, about 3 minutes. Stir in the flour, just to combine.

5. In a medium bowl, whisk together the egg yolks, milk, rum, and vanilla. Stir the egg mixture into the flour mixture until blended.

6. In another large bowl, with clean beaters beat the egg whites with the salt on low speed until foamy. Increase the speed and beat until soft peaks form, about 4 minutes. Gently fold the whites into the rest of the batter. Pour the batter over the fruit in the baking dish and bake 25 minutes or until the top is golden and firm to the touch.

7. Serve warm or at room temperature, sprinkled with confectioner's sugar.

Warm Fruit Compote

Composta di Frutta Calda

Makes 6 to 8 servings

Rum is often used to flavor desserts in Italy. Dark rum has a deeper flavor than light rum. Substitute another liqueur or a sweet wine such as Marsala for the rum in this recipe if you like. Or make a nonalcoholic version with orange or apple juice.

2 firm ripe pears, peeled and cored

1 golden delicious or Granny Smith apple, peeled and cored

1 cup pitted prunes

1 cup dried figs, stem ends removed

½ cup dried pitted apricots

½ cup dark raisins

¼ cup sugar

2 (2-inch) strips lemon zest

1 cup water

½ cup dark rum

1. Cut the pears and apple into 8 wedges. Cut the wedges into bite-size pieces.

2. Combine all of the ingredients in a large saucepan. Cover and bring to a simmer over medium-low heat. Cook until the fresh fruits are tender and the dried fruits are plump, about 20 minutes. Add a little more water if they seem dry.

3. Let cool slightly before serving or cover and refrigerate up to 3 days.

Venetian Caramelized Fruit

Golosezzi Veneziani

Makes 8 servings

The caramel coating on these Venetian skewered fruits hardens, with a result something like a candy apple. Pat the fruits thoroughly dry and make these fruit skewers on a dry day. If the weather is humid, the caramel will not harden properly.

1 tangerine or clementine, peeled, divided into sections

8 small strawberries, hulled

8 seedless grapes

8 pitted dates

1 cup sugar

½ cup light corn syrup

¼ cup water

1. Thread the fruit pieces alternately on each of eight 6-inch wood skewers. Set a wire cooling rack on top of a tray.

2. In a skillet large enough to fit the skewers into lengthwise, combine the sugar, corn syrup, and water. Cook over medium heat, stirring occasionally until the sugar is completely dissolved, about 3 minutes. When the mixture begins to boil, stop stirring and cook until the syrup starts to brown around the edges. Then gently swirl the pan over the heat until the syrup is an even golden brown, about 2 minutes more.

3. Remove the pan from the heat. Using tongs, quickly dip each skewer in the syrup, turning to coat the fruit lightly but thoroughly. Let the excess syrup drain back into the pan. Place the skewers on the rack to cool. (If the syrup in the pan hardens before all of the skewers have been dipped, reheat it gently.) Serve at room temperature within 2 hours.

Fruit with Honey and Grappa

Composta di Frutta alla Grappa

Makes 6 servings

Grappa is a kind of brandy made from vinaccia, the skins and seeds that are left after grapes are pressed to make wine. At one time, grappa was a coarse beverage mostly drunk in northern Italy by farmhands and laborers for warmth on cold winter days. Today, grappa is a very refined drink, sold in designer bottles with ornate stoppers. Some grappas are flavored with fruit or herbs, while others are aged in wood casks. Use a simple, unflavored grappa for this fruit salad and for other cooking purposes.

$\frac{1}{3}$ cup honey

$\frac{1}{3}$ cup grappa, brandy, or fruit liqueur

1 tablespoon fresh lemon juice

2 kiwis, peeled and sliced

2 navel oranges, peeled and cut into wedges

1 pint strawberries, sliced

1 cup halved seedless green grapes

2 medium bananas, sliced

1. In a large serving bowl, mix together the honey, grappa, and lemon juice.

2. Stir in the kiwis, oranges, strawberries, and grapes. Chill for at least 1 hour or up to 4 hours. Stir in the bananas just before serving.

Winter Fruit Salad

Macedonia del' Inverno

Makes 6 servings

In Italy, a fruit salad is called Macedonia, because that country was once divided up into many little sections that were brought together to make a whole, just as the salad is made up of bite-size pieces of different fruits. In the winter, when fruit choices are limited, Italians make salads like this one dressed with honey and lemon juice. As a variation, substitute apricot jam or orange marmalade for the honey.

3 tablespoons honey

3 tablespoons orange juice

1 tablespoon fresh lemon juice

2 grapefruits, peeled and separated into wedges

2 kiwis, peeled and sliced

2 ripe pears

2 cups seedless green grapes, halved lengthwise

1. In a large bowl, mix together the honey, orange juice, and lemon
juice.

2. Add the fruits to the bowl and toss well. Chill for at least 1 hour
or up to 4 hours before serving.

Grilled Summer Fruit

Spiedini alla Frutta

Makes 6 servings

Grilled summer fruits are great for a barbecue. Serve them plain or with slices of sponge cake and ice cream.

If using wood skewers, soak them in cold water at least 30 minutes to prevent burning.

2 nectarines, cut into 1-inch chunks

2 plums, cut into 1-inch chunks

2 pears, cut into 1-inch chunks

2 apricots, cut into quarters

2 bananas, cut into 1-inch chunks

Fresh mint leaves

About 2 tablespoons sugar

1. Place a barbecue grill or broiler rack about 5 inches away from the heat source. Preheat the grill or broiler.

2. Alternate pieces of the fruits with the mint leaves on 6 skewers. Sprinkle with the sugar.

3. Grill or broil the fruit 3 minutes on one side. Turn the skewers and grill or broil until lightly browned, about 2 minutes more. Serve hot.

Warm Ricotta with Honey

Ricotta al Miele

Makes 2 to 3 servings

The success of this dessert depends on the quality of the ricotta, so buy the freshest available. While part-skimmed-milk ricotta is fine, the fat-free is very grainy and tasteless, so don't use it. If you like, add some fresh fruit, or try raisins and a pinch of cinnamon.

1 cup whole-milk ricotta

2 tablespoons honey

1. Place the ricotta in a small bowl set over a smaller pan of simmering water. Heat until warm, about 10 minutes. Stir well.

2. Scoop the ricotta into serving dishes. Drizzle with the honey. Serve immediately.

Coffee Ricotta

Ricotta all' Caffè

Makes 2 to 3 servings

Here is a quick dessert that lends itself to a multitude of variations. Serve it with some plain butter cookies.

If you can't buy finely ground espresso, be sure to run the grounds through your coffee grinder or food processor. If the grounds are too large, the dessert won't blend right, leaving it with a gritty texture.

1 cup (8 ounces) whole or part-skim ricotta

1 tablespoon finely ground (espresso) coffee

1 tablespoon sugar

Chocolate shavings

In a medium bowl, whisk together the ricotta, espresso, and sugar until the mixture is smooth and the sugar is dissolved. (For a creamier texture, mix the ingredients in a food processor.) Spoon into parfait glasses or goblets and top with chocolate shavings. Serve immediately.

Variation: For chocolate ricotta, substitute 1 tablespoon unsweetened cocoa for the coffee.

Mascarpone and Peaches

Mascarpone al Pesche

Makes 6 servings

Smooth, creamy mascarpone and peaches with crunchy amaretti look beautiful in parfait or wine glasses. Serve this dessert at a dinner party. No one will guess how easy it is to make.

1 cup (8 ounces) mascarpone

¼ cup sugar

1 tablespoon fresh lemon juice

1 cup very cold whipping cream

3 peaches or nectarines, peeled and cut into bite-size pieces

⅓ cup orange liqueur, amaretto, or rum

8 amaretti cookies, crushed into crumbs (about ½ cup)

2 tablespoons toasted sliced almonds

1. At least 20 minutes before you are ready to make the dessert, place a large bowl and the beaters of an electric mixer in the refrigerator.

2. When ready, in a medium bowl, whisk together the mascarpone, sugar, and lemon juice. Remove the bowl and beaters from the refrigerator. Pour the cream into the chilled bowl and whip the cream at high speed until it holds its shape softly when the beaters are lifted, about 4 minutes. With a spatula, gently fold the whipped cream into the mascarpone mixture.

3. In a medium bowl, toss together the peaches and liqueur.

4. Spoon half of the mascarpone cream into six parfait glasses or wine goblets. Make a layer of the peaches, then sprinkle with the amaretti crumbs. Top with the remaining cream. Cover and chill in the refrigerator up to 2 hours.

5. Sprinkle with the almonds before serving.

Chocolate Foam with Raspberries

Spuma di Cioccolato al Lampone

Makes 8 servings

Whipped cream folded into mascarpone and chocolate is like an instant chocolate mousse. The raspberries are a sweet and tangy complement.

1 pint raspberries

1 to 2 tablespoons sugar

2 tablespoons raspberry, cherry, or orange liqueur

3 ounces bittersweet or semisweet chocolate

½ cup (4 ounces) mascarpone, at room temperature

2 cups chilled heavy or whipping cream

Chocolate shavings, for garnish

1. At least 20 minutes before you are ready to make the dessert, place a large bowl and the beaters of an electric mixer in the refrigerator.

2. When ready, toss the raspberries with the sugar and liqueur in a
medium bowl. Set aside.

3. Fill a small pot with an inch of water. Bring it to a simmer over
low heat. Place the chocolate in a bowl larger than the rim of the
pot and set the bowl over the simmering water. Let stand until
the chocolate is melted. Remove from the heat and stir the
chocolate until smooth. Let cool slightly, about 15 minutes. With
a rubber spatula, fold in the mascarpone.

4. Remove the chilled bowl and beaters from the refrigerator. Pour
the cream into the bowl and whip the cream at high speed until
it holds its shape softly when the beaters are lifted, about 4
minutes.

5. With a spatula, gently fold half of the cream into the chocolate
mixture, reserving the second half for the topping.

6. Spoon half of the chocolate cream into eight parfait glasses.
Layer with the raspberries. Spoon on the remaining chocolate
cream. Top with the whipped cream. Garnish with the chocolate
shavings. Serve immediately.

Tiramisù

Tiramisù

Makes 8 to 10 servings

No one is quite sure why this dessert is called "pick me up" in Italian, but it is assumed the name comes from the jolt of caffeine it provides from the coffee and chocolate. While the classic version contains raw egg yolks mixed in with the mascarpone, my version is eggless because I do not like the flavor of raw eggs and find they make the dessert heavier than it needs to be.

Savoiardi—crisp ladyfingers imported from Italy—are widely available, but ordinary lady fingers or slices of plain cake can be substituted. If you like, add a couple of tablespoons of rum or cognac to the coffee.

1 cup chilled heavy or whipping cream

1 pound mascarpone

⅓ cup sugar

24 savoiardi (imported Italian ladyfingers)

1 cup brewed espresso coffee at room temperature

2 tablespoons unsweetened cocoa powder

1. At least 20 minutes before you are ready to make the dessert, place a large bowl and the beaters of an electric mixer in the refrigerator.

2. When ready, remove the bowl and beaters from the refrigerator. Pour the cream into the bowl and whip the cream at high speed until it holds its shape softly when the beaters are lifted, about 4 minutes.

3. In a large bowl, whisk together the mascarpone and sugar until smooth. Take about one third of the whipped cream, and with a flexible spatula, gently fold it into the mascarpone mixture to lighten it. Carefully fold in the remaining cream.

4. Lightly and quickly dip half of the savoiardi in the coffee. (Do not saturate them or they will fall apart.) Arrange the cookies in a single layer in a 9 × 2–inch square or round serving dish. Spoon on half of the mascarpone cream.

5. Dip the remaining savoiardi in the coffee and arrange them in a layer over the mascarpone. Top with the remaining mascarpone mixture and spread it smooth with the spatula. Place the cocoa in a fine-mesh strainer and shake it over the top of the dessert. Cover with foil or plastic wrap and refrigerate 3 to 4 hours or overnight so that the flavors can meld. It will keep well in the refrigerator up to 24 hours.

Strawberry Tiramisù

Tiramisù alle Fragole

Makes 8 servings

Here is a strawberry version of tiramisù that I came across in an Italian cooking magazine. I like it even better than the coffee version, but then I favor fruit-based desserts of all kinds.

Maraschino is a clear, slightly bitter Italian cherry liqueur named for the marasche variety of cherries. Maraschino is available here, but you can substitute another fruit liqueur if you prefer.

3 pints strawberries, washed and hulled

½ cup orange juice

¼ cup maraschino, crème di cassis, or orange liqueur

¼ cup sugar

1 cup chilled heavy or whipping cream

8 ounces mascarpone

24 savoiardi (Italian lady fingers)

1. Set aside 2 cups of the best-looking strawberries for garnish. Chop the remainder. In a large bowl, combine the strawberries with the orange juice, liqueur, and sugar. Let stand at room temperature 1 hour.

2. Meanwhile, place a large bowl and the beaters of an electric mixer in the refrigerator. When ready, remove the bowl and beaters from the refrigerator. Pour the cream into the bowl and whip the cream at high speed until it holds its shape softly when the beaters are lifted, about 4 minutes. With a flexible spatula, gently fold in the mascarpone.

3. Make a layer of ladyfingers in a 9 × 2–inch square or round serving dish. Spoon on half of the strawberries and their juice. Spread half of the mascarpone cream over the berries.

4. Repeat with a second layer of ladyfingers, strawberries, and cream, spreading the cream smooth with a spatula. Cover and refrigerate 3 to 4 hours or overnight so that the flavors can meld.

5. Just before serving, slice the remaining strawberries and arrange them in rows on top.

Italian Trifle

Zuppa Inglese

Makes 10 to 12 servings

"English soup" is the whimsical name for this lush dessert. It is believed that Italian cooks borrowed the idea from English trifle and added Italian touches.

1 Vin Santo Rings or 1 (12-ounce) store-bought pound cake, cut into slices, $\frac{1}{4}$ inch thick

$\frac{1}{2}$ cup sour cherry or raspberrry jam

$\frac{1}{2}$ cup dark rum or orange liqueur

$2\frac{1}{2}$ cups each Chocolate and Vanilla Pastry Cream

1 cup heavy or whipping cream

Fresh raspberries, for garnish

Chocolate shavings, for garnish

1. Prepare the sponge cake and pastry creams, if necessary. Then, in a small bowl, stir together the jam and rum.

2. Spoon half of the vanilla pastry cream into the bottom of a 3-quart serving bowl. Place $^1/_4$ of the cake slices on top and brush with $^1/_4$ of the jam mixture. Spoon half of the chocolate pastry cream on top.

3. Make another layer of $^1/_4$ of the cake and jam mixture. Repeat with the remaining vanilla cream, $^1/_4$ of the remaining cake and jam mixture, chocolate cream, and the rest of the cake and jam mixture. Cover tightly with plastic and refrigerate at least 3 hours and up to 24 hours.

4. At least 20 minutes before serving, place a large bowl and the beaters of an electric mixer in the refrigerator. Just before serving, remove the bowl and beaters from the refrigerator. Pour the cream into the bowl and whip at high speed until it holds its shape softly when the beaters are lifted, about 4 minutes.

5. Spoon the cream on top of the trifle. Garnish with raspberries and chocolate shavings.

Zabaglione

Makes 2 servings

In Italy, zabaglione (pronounced tsah-bahl-yo-neh; the g is silent) is a sweet, creamy, egg-based dessert, often served as a strength-building tonic for someone suffering from a cold or other ailment. Illness or no illness, it is a delicious dessert on its own or as a sauce for fruit or cake.

Zabaglione should be eaten as soon as it is made, or it can collapse. To make zabaglione ahead of time, see the recipe for chilled zabaglione.

3 large egg yolks

3 tablespoons sugar

3 tablespoons dry or sweet Marsala or vin santo

1. In the bottom half of a double boiler or in a medium saucepan, bring about 2 inches of water to a simmer.

2. In the top half of the double boiler or in a heatproof bowl that fits comfortably over the saucepan, beat the egg yolks and sugar with a hand-held electric mixer on medium speed until light, about 2 minutes. Blend in the Marsala. Place the mixture over

the simmering water. (Do not allow the water to boil, or the eggs will scramble.)

3. While it warms over the simmering water, continue to beat the egg mixture until it is pale yellow and very fluffy and holds a soft shape when dropped from the beaters, 3 to 5 minutes.

4. Spoon into tall goblets and serve immediately.

Chocolate Zabaglione

Zabaglione al Cioccolato

Makes 4 servings

This variation on zabaglione is like a rich chocolate mousse. Serve it warm with cool whipped cream.

3 ounces bittersweet or semisweet chocolate, chopped

¼ cup heavy cream

4 large egg yolks

¼ cup sugar

2 tablespoons rum or amaretto liqueur

1. In the bottom half of a double boiler or in a medium saucepan, bring about 2 inches of water to a simmer. Combine the chocolate and cream in a small heatproof bowl set over the simmering water. Let stand until the chocolate is melted. Stir with a flexible spatula until smooth. Remove from the heat.

2. In the top of the double boiler or in another heatproof bowl that fits over the saucepan, beat the egg yolks and sugar with a hand-held electric mixer until light, about 2 minutes. Blend in the rum. Place the mixture over the simmering water. (Do not allow the water to boil, or the eggs will scramble.)

3. Beat the yolk mixture until it is pale and fluffy and holds a soft shape when dropped from the beaters, 3 to 5 minutes. Remove from the heat.

4. With a rubber spatula, gently fold in the chocolate mixture. Serve immediately.

Chilled Zabaglione with Berries

Zabaglione Freddo con Frutti di Bosco

Makes 6 servings

If you don't want to make zabaglione right before serving, this cold version is a good alternative. The zabaglione is cooled in an ice-water bath, then folded into whipped cream. It can be made up to 24 hours ahead. I like to serve it over fresh berries or ripe figs.

1 recipe (about 1½ cups) Zabaglione

¾ cup chilled heavy or whipping cream

2 tablespoons confectioner's sugar

1 tablespoon orange liqueur

1½ cups blueberries, raspberries, or a combination, rinsed and patted dry

1. At least 20 minutes before you are ready to make the zabaglione, place a large bowl and the beaters of an electric mixer in the refrigerator. Fill another large bowl with ice and water.

2. Prepare the zabaglione through step 3. As soon as the zabaglione is finished, remove it from the simmering water and set the bowl over the ice water. With a wire whisk, beat the zabaglione until it is cold, about 3 minutes.

3. Remove the chilled bowl and beaters from the refrigerator. Pour the cream into the bowl and whip the cream at high speed until it begins to hold a soft shape, about 2 minutes. Add the confectioner's sugar and orange liqueur. Whip the cream until it holds a soft shape when the beaters are lifted, about 2 minutes more. With a flexible spatula, gently fold in the chilled zabaglione. Cover and chill in the refrigerator at least 1 hour until ready to serve.

4. Divide the berries among 6 serving dishes. Top with the chilled zabaglione cream and serve immediately.

Lemon Gelatin

Gelatina di Limone

Makes 6 servings

Lemon juice and zest make this dessert light and refreshing.

2 envelopes unflavored gelatin

1 cup sugar

2½ cups cold water

2 (2-inch) strips lemon zest

⅔ cup fresh lemon juice

Lemon slices and mint sprigs, for garnish

1. In a medium saucepan, stir together the gelatin and sugar. Add the water and lemon zest. Cook over medium heat, stirring constantly, until the gelatin is completely dissolved, about 3 minutes. (Do not allow the mixture to boil.)

2. Remove from the heat and stir in the lemon juice. Pour the mixture through a fine-mesh strainer into a 5-cup mold or bowl. Cover and chill until set, 4 hours up to overnight.

3. When ready to serve, fill a bowl with warm water and dip the
mold into the water for 30 seconds. Run a small knife around the
sides. Lay a plate over the mold, and holding them together,
invert them both so that the gelatin transfers to the plate.
Garnish with lemon slices and mint sprigs.

Orange Rum Gelatin

Gelatina di Arancia al Rhum

Makes 4 servings

Rum-scented whipped cream is a nice accompaniment. Blood orange juice works best here.

2 envelopes unflavored gelatin

½ cup sugar

½ cup cold water

3 cups fresh orange juice

2 tablespoons dark rum

Orange slices, for garnish

1. In a medium saucepan, stir together the gelatin and sugar. Add the water and cook over medium heat, stirring constantly, until the gelatin is completely dissolved, about 3 minutes. (Do not allow the mixture to boil.)

2. Remove from the heat and stir in orange juice and rum. Pour mixture into a 5-cup mold or bowl. Cover and chill until set, 4 hours up to overnight.

3. When ready to serve, fill a bowl with warm water and dip the mold into the water for 30 seconds. Run a small knife around the sides. Lay a plate over the mold, and holding them together, invert them both so that the gelatin transfers to the plate. Garnish with the orange slices.

Espresso Gelatin

Gelatina di Caffè

Makes 4 servings

When I first tasted this coffee gelatin in Milan, it was served with both whipped cream and Chilled Zabaglione, a dazzling combination. This is also refreshing, light, and delicious on its own.

2 envelopes unflavored gelatin

1 cup sugar

2½ cup cold water

2 tablespoons instant espresso powder

1. In a medium saucepan, stir together the gelatin and sugar. Add the water and cook over medium heat, stirring constantly, until the gelatin is completely dissolved, about 3 minutes. Do not allow the mixture to boil.

2. Remove from the heat. Stir in the instant coffee. Pour the mixture into a 1-quart mold. Cover and chill until set, 4 hours up to overnight.

3. When ready to serve, fill a bowl with warm water and dip the

mold into the water for 30 seconds. Run a small knife around the

sides. Lay a plate over the mold, and holding them together,

invert them so the gelatin transfers to the plate.

Panna Cotta

Makes 6 servings

The best version of this dessert I have had was in Piedmont at the Giardino da Felicin, a favorite restaurant in Monforte d'Alba. It had just been made and was barely gelled. When I touched it with my spoon, its shape yielded smoothly. The dessert melted in my mouth and tasted of nothing but the finest sweet, fresh cream.

The name of this Piedmontese dessert means "cooked cream," though there is practically no cooking involved. A fresh berry sauce or warm chocolate sauce goes well with it, or just some fresh fruit.

1 envelope unflavored gelatin

1½ cups whole milk

1½ cups heavy or whipping cream

1 vanilla bean or 2 teaspoons pure vanilla extract

1 (2-inch) strip lemon zest

¼ cup sugar

    Fresh Strawberry Sauce

1. Sprinkle the gelatin over the milk and let stand 2 minutes until the gelatin absorbs some of the liquid and softens.

2. In a medium saucepan, combine the cream, vanilla bean (if using vanilla extract, reserve until later), lemon zest, and sugar. Bring to a simmer over medium heat. Add the gelatin mixture and cook, stirring frequently, until the gelatin is completely dissolved, about 3 minutes.

3. Remove the vanilla bean and lemon zest with a slotted spoon. Slit the vanilla bean lengthwise with a small sharp knife and scrape the seeds out. Stir the seeds into the cream mixture. (Or add the vanilla extract, if using.)

4. Pour the cream into a large bowl. Fill a larger bowl with ice and set the bowl with the cream in the ice. Let the cream cool, stirring frequently, until it begins to set, about 10 minutes. Pour the cream into 6 individual custard cups. Cover and chill until set, 4 hours up to overnight.

5. Prepare the strawberry sauce, if necessary. When ready to serve, briefly dip the bottom of the cups in a bowl filled with warm water to loosen. Run a small knife around the inside of the cups. Invert the cups onto serving plates. Spoon the sauce over each and serve.